P9-CKL-612

DATE DUE

Selection
and Evaluation
of
Electronic Resources

Selection
and Evaluation
of
Electronic Resources

Gail K. Dickinson

1994
LIBRARIES UNLIMITED, INC.
Englewood, Colorado

LIBRARIES UNLIMITED, INC.
P.O. Box 6633
Englewood, CO 80155-6633
1-800-237-6124

Library of Congress Cataloging-in-Publication Data

Dickinson, Gail K.
    Selection and evaluation of electronic resources / Gail K.
Dickinson.
    xi, 103 p. 17x25 cm.
    Includes bibliographical references.
    ISBN 1-56308-098-2
    1. Data base selection. I. Title.
Z688.D38D53   1994
025.04--dc20   93-43935
                                                    CIP

To Maggie and Beth Ann,
for giving me balance.

Contents

Preface

I wrote this book to offer some criteria for the selection of electronic resources, based on my experiences in the past several years of assisting with that selection process. This book will not answer many of the questions that librarians will have about electronic technology. It will not give a "top ten" list of CD-ROMs or suggest any one technology over another.

The fact is that all libraries are different. We serve different populations, with diverse needs. If every library made a top ten list of the resources that best served its populations, I would hope that the lists would all be different.

It's not the technology, or the number of computers, or how many CD-ROMs a library has that make it a good library. Instead, the measure of a library has to do with the level of service to the patron community.

I hope that it will help those entering the electronic resources field to base choices on the benefit of the resource to users, rather than the sophistication of the technology. A computer in a library does not automatically improve the level of service to patrons, but a well-chosen electronic resource can change the life of the library forever.

In fact, there is no list of "must-have" electronic resources that will be automatic purchases. There are only questions to ask, criteria to weigh, and, in the end, selection decisions to make.

I hope this book will help with these decisions.

I gratefully acknowledge the support of the school board and administration of Union-Endicott Central School District, particularly Superintendent Dennis M. Sweeney and Assistant Superintendent Joseph N. Marzo, for their support of the library program that made this learning possible.

My thanks to the vendors and producers of electronic products, for their generosity with their products and permissions.

A special thanks to building-level librarians everywhere and especially in Union-Endicott, who work to implement electronic resources for the betterment of their program and to the benefit of their patrons.

1

Introduction

One of the most dramatic changes in libraries has been the introduction of computers. These electronic information resources have drastically altered the way patrons use libraries. The change is universal, as academic, public, school, and special libraries are now implementing electronic resources to complement their library programs.

Electronic resources are often regarded as essential; a library could hardly be considered providing excellent service without the full range of electronic information resources. Unlike the audio-visual (AV) or microfiche departments, which are usually squirreled away in a back corner of the library, electronic resources are readily available to patrons as part of the library reference area.

Although printed texts will always be a part of a library, information is now available in a wide range of formats. These are commonly divided into three categories: print, non-print, and electronic. Print resources are books, journals, and other textual information. Non-print refers to audio-visual and other materials not in text form. Electronic resources can be defined as resources that are accessed by or read from a computer. Electronic resources include CD-ROM disks, online data-

THE WORLD OF INFORMATION SOURCES
Print: books, journals, other printed text
Non-print: audio-visual and other non-print media
Electronic: information accessed by a computer or read from a computer screen

bases, hard-disk-resident databases, and other resources found on computers. When electronic resources first began appearing in libraries in the late 1970s and early 1980s, there was little choice among types. "Should we offer online searching service to patrons?" was the question, not "Which online service makes the best sense for our patrons?" Even when CD-ROM products appeared, the choice was whether or not to offer a CD-ROM encyclopedia, not *which* one to offer, because one product, the Grolier Electronic Encyclopedia, was alone on the market for several years. Now the decision is not so simple—librarians must choose from among a wide variety of options. In order to select the best resource, the library staff must be aware of the underlying theory of electronic databases and understand the impact electronic resources can have on a library program.

DATABASE DEFINITION

Electronic resources are databases that the computer searches at the command of the user. Essentially, a database can be thought of as a collection of pieces of information, much like a folder in which papers are filed. Usually, the information centers around a certain theme or subject. If one's desk is littered with papers, the first step in sorting out the mess might be to separate the papers into piles of information with similar characteristics. Each pile could be considered a database. A telephone book is a good example of a database: The entries have a specific purpose, and each entry is unique. In a database, a single, complete piece of information is called a *record*. Each part that makes up the complete record is called a *field*. In a telephone book, the name, address, and telephone number are the fields that make up the record. The number of fields depends on how far the records can be divided into separate units. It is feasible in a phone book to have fields for telephone number, first name, last name, street address, and city (see fig. 1.1).

Smith, Darlene   365 Hughes Ave   Oakville   555-2432

1 record in a sample telephone book. Note fields:
NAME,   STREET,   CITY,   and   TELEPHONE NUMBER.

Fig. 1.1. Database Example: Telephone Book Listing.

In a print database, only a few fields can be searched. In a print telephone book, for example, each number can easily be looked up only by the person's or organization's name. If a patron only knows the telephone number or the address but not the name, however, finding the number would require reading the telephone book. Of course, the telephone book could be printed various ways. Imagine the versatility of a telephone book if it were printed in three parts. The first section could be alphabetical by name, the second part numerically by telephone number, and the third part alphabetical by street. With an electronic database, that kind of versatility is basic and very easily accomplished.

In a traditional library card catalog, the "pile of information" is the list of materials in the library collection. The fields that can be searched are author, title, and subject. Even though the search can be conducted in three different ways, however, the search is still limited to the strict alphabetic list. Knowing some, but not all, of the title destines a search to failure, especially if the only part of the title that is known is the last few words. In an electronic database, that kind of search is not at all difficult; the potential exists to search every field in the record. Think of a telephone book in which a patron can input a telephone number and find out the organization's name and address. Think of a reference desk where a librarian can help a patron find a phone number when all the patron knows about the person she wants to call is that her name is Maggie and she lives on Yale Street. This is the kind of searching power an electronic database can provide.

An electronic database can also be searched for any words contained in a given field. This is especially helpful in an electronic library catalog when a patron can remember only a part of the title. This is called *word searching*. In word searching, the computer looks anywhere in a specified field for an exact match of a word or combination of words specified by the user. Word searching is not available in every electronic resource, but it is an extremely important consideration when making a purchase. Electronic resources have the potential to provide total access to information. Purchasing an electronic resource without word searching capability limits that potential.

Before a database can be searched, the fields must be indexed. Usually, the producer of the database will decide which fields to index; it is rare that all fields would be indexed. For instance, the field containing the number of pages in each book is rarely indexed in a library catalog. The librarian will have to decide if searching that field is an important consideration. Does the average library patron have a need to search the collection for every book containing less than 200 pages? For the 16-year-old library patron looking for a quick read for a book report, that answer could well be "yes." When purchasing an electronic database, the librarian should consider the list of available fields in the database and how many of those fields are indexed. Theoretically, all words input into an electronic database can be searched. In reality, however, a database rarely has that extensive an index, and each database has words that are not indexed. These words are sometimes called *stop words*. Each database vendor has a different list of stop words, and each vendor may refer to them by a different name. Usually, these are small words such as *a*, *of*, and *the*. This concept of ignoring common words in an index should be very familiar to users of the standard print library card catalog. A traditional card catalog has its own list of stop words: *A*, *an*, and *the* are not indexed when used at the beginning of a title. Stop words are not indexed because of the number of times the words would appear in the field and the amount of space the words would take up in the index. If a print card catalog used the word *the* at the beginning of a title, these titles would take up several drawers, and patrons would face time-consuming and frustrating searches.

Libraries have databases in various forms. A book can be considered a database—a database made up of a single record. The fields in that record would be a small field for the author, another small field for the title, for the publisher, the copyright date, and so on. The largest field would be for the text of the book, which would contain many thousands of words.

Database Types

In library systems, four main kinds of databases are recognized: full-text, bibliographic, directory, and numeric. A library of any size contains examples of each kind of database, and each is used for different purposes. Generally speaking, though, all four types are searched in the same way.

Full-Text

A full-text database contains all the information available for a certain record. Think of an encyclopedia as an example. Each article is complete, containing all of the information that fits under a specific topic. Some databases—the Gutenberg Project, for example—are now making full texts of classic novels such as *Peter Pan* and *Alice in Wonderland* available through computer networks. Other databases have complete magazine articles or the complete texts of newspapers.

The advantages of searching full-text databases is that the patron has all of the information in one source. With a printer attached to the computer, the patron can print out an entire magazine article without going to the library shelves to find the magazine or retrieving it through interlibrary loan. Being able to search the full text of newspapers, another fast-growing electronic source, provides patrons with incredible flexibility.

One disadvantage of full-text searching is that the library must consider the cost of computer paper. Even if each patron only prints two or three short articles of a few pages in length each, that still means that each patron will be printing six to ten pages. Each patron will spend more time at the computer doing a search—it takes less time to review a citation or an abstract than to review a full-text article. A patron using a full-text source will use only a fraction of the number of references that a patron using another type of database will use.

Full-text databases are also much harder to search than other types because finding a word used in text is much less specific than finding a word used in a subject heading. However, because of the convenience of having the complete material readily at hand, full-text databases are probably the fastest growing database category.

Bibliographic

Bibliographic databases give citations containing author, title, publisher, date of publication, and so forth. A bibliographic database may also include abstracts along with the citation. An index to magazine articles is an example of a bibliographic database.

The advantage to using a bibliographic database is that it enables fast searches, and the patron walks away from the computer with a list of references. The patron can then select the most pertinent references, retrieve them from the stacks or magazine files, and review them at leisure. While that patron is reviewing the printout, another patron is making use of the computer.

The disadvantage of a bibliographic database is that a library will probably not have in its collection all of the materials listed in the database. Patrons will most likely use interlibrary loan to retrieve resources not available through the initial library.

Directory

A directory database has simple lists of information. The telephone book is an example of a directory database. The advantage of an electronic directory database is that the list can be searched in a variety of ways.

Numeric

A numeric database contains numeric data on a certain subject. This data may be stock market information, population or census figures, and so on. Some numeric database information can be printed in chart or table form.

Most of the databases in a library are either full-text or bibliographic. Some of the same resources are available in both full-text and bibliographic form. The librarian making a purchase decision will have to weigh the pros and cons of each very carefully and visualize both the intended uses and the frequency of use to determine the wisest purchase for a library program.

FOUR TYPES OF DATABASES
1. Full-text: all text pertaining to a record
2. Bibliographic: citations or abstracts only
3. Directory: lists
4. Numeric: numeric data

THE WORLD OF ELECTRONIC RESOURCES

There are a variety of electronic resources available to libraries and many ways to package these resources. A library may place a database on the hard disk of the computer, purchase a CD-ROM, invest in a modem for online searching, or even retrieve information via cable television or satellite. Regardless of the manner in which they are packaged, all databases are generally similar in definition and in the ways that they are searched by the user.

Hard-Disk-Resident Databases

Hard-disk-resident databases are purchased by the library on 5¼- or 3½-inch disks. The data is then transferred in its entirety to the hard drive of the computer. Obviously, the size of the database is limited by the size of the hard drive of the computer. Because no extra equipment is needed, this is an inexpensive way to obtain databases for patron searching.

Libraries can also create their own databases of local collections and place them on the hard disk for patron or librarian use. The computer software to create locally produced databases is available commercially, and some libraries make this available to patrons so they can compose their own databases.

The hard disk of a computer can be used in a different way. When a database is too large to fit on floppy disks, it is sometimes placed on tape drives. Miniframe or mainframe computers have large reserves of memory, so it is possible to purchase the tapes of databases that are otherwise only available on CD or online and transfer them to the hard drive. These databases can be used not only by library patrons but also by anyone who is logged on to the large computer from a remote location via modem. In this way colleges and universities can take resources that previously were only available in the library on a few workstations and give patrons access from anywhere on campus or in the community.

Online Databases

Installing a modem for a computer and connecting it to a telephone line allows library patrons to log on to databases that are resident in other computers. These computers are usually large mainframes and can be located across the street, across the country, or across the world. Online databases may be university library catalogs or databases provided by government agencies such as NASA or the National Library of Medicine. Online databases may be any of the four types of databases.

Mainframe computers may contain just one database or several hundred. There are information vendors that have collections of databases on their computers. A library may log on to that computer, which is quite large, and then have a choice of hundreds of databases. Dialog Information Services and BRS Technologies are examples of such information companies, usually referred to as *supermarket vendors* because they offer such a wide variety of resources.

CD-ROM Databases

By connecting a CD-ROM player to a computer, a library may begin to use databases contained on laser-encoded disks. The acronym *CD-ROM* stands for *compact disk-read only memory*, which means the patron cannot change the information once it has been encoded. CD-ROM technology is an exploding field within the library world. The databases available on CD-ROM grow in number and type each year. Encyclopedias, magazine indexes, and tremendous amounts of full-text data are currently available in this format.

Most of the reference sources on CD-ROM fit on one disk, but there are a few that must use several disks. The amount of information a computer floppy disk or CD-ROM disk can hold is measured in megabytes. A CD-ROM disk can hold about 500 megabytes. A typical home computer may hold 30 to 40 megabytes.

All CD-ROMs come with software that must be loaded onto the hard drive of the computer. This is sometimes referred to as the *search engine*, or *front-end software.* This software gives the computer the necessary instructions to retrieve information from the disk.

Other Types of Databases

There are other types of databases available for library use besides the main types listed above. For example, some databases can be accessed via satellite. The X•PRESS service offers this capability in many locations through the local cable television company. A small box beside the computer ties into a local cable television line and translates that signal into a format that can be read by a computer. The stream of information read by the computer can be searched by keyword and stored in the computer.

ELECTRONIC INFORMATION RESOURCES
1. Hard-disk-resident: stored on the hard drive of the computer
2. Online: accessed through a modem and telephone line
3. CD-ROM: stored on a laser-encoded disk
4. Other: satellite and other sources

IMPLEMENTATION

When electronic resources are added to a library program, the impact is tremendous. Electronic databases greatly increase access to information and can make the tedious and time-consuming task of beginning research much easier. With the variety of databases available and the limited amount of financial resources that libraries have, however, the implementation must be carefully planned to ensure optimal use of space, money, and time.

A well-planned electronic resources program will offer CD-ROM, online, hard-disk-resident, and all other kinds of databases. The size of the library is not a factor. In an extremely small library, all of the above resources can be made available through a single computer. A single database can even be available in both print format and a variety of electronic formats. The choices are endless and must be considered in light of the function of the library, the number of patrons in the library at any one time, and the age and education of patrons.

Selection of electronic resources must be considered as thoroughly as selection of any other resource added to the library. It is doubtful that a library would consider adding an expensive reference book that had wonderful pictures but would only offer very limited value to library patrons. In the same way, the fact that a resource is in electronic form does not necessarily make it valuable to a library collection. An electronic resource with flashy pictures and electronic gadgets must also be considered in the light of the following questions.

What Patrons Will Use It? In a school or academic library, it is assumed that the resource has a direct link to the curriculum. In a public or special library, by contrast, the librarian must take into consideration the interests of the patrons it serves. The information referenced in the database must still be read; therefore, the difficulty of the materials must be considered. A good rule of thumb is to think back over the past year. If this resource had been in place, who would have used it, and how often?

How Many Patrons Have a Use for This? Generally speaking, every library will want an encyclopedia and a magazine index in some electronic form. All libraries have these in the print form, but they will be just as valuable and be used much more often in the electronic form. Once a library gets past these basic resources and into the more specific kinds of databases, the interests and research needs of the patrons must be considered in more detail.

How Often Will It Be Used? Will this resource be in demand by many patrons at the same time? Is it a subject that is studied in depth at one time of the year and then not studied at all at other times? These are important considerations when determining whether to purchase a resource on CD-ROM or to log on to it as an online database.

What Effect Will It Have on Other Resources? When electronic resources are included in a library, patrons tend to use a wide variety of resources. The patron who laboriously copied three citations from a print magazine index will now print fifteen, twenty, or even more citations from an electronic source. Interlibrary loans may double or even triple with the advent of electronic resources. A future consideration may be to purchase full-text sources so patrons can have instantaneous delivery of information along with instantaneous access.

INITIAL CONSIDERATIONS FOR PURCHASING ELECTRONIC RESOURCES
1. What will patrons search?
2. Which patrons will use it?
3. How often will it be used?
4. How will it affect the total program?
5. How difficult will the training be?

TRAINING

Training the library staff in the use of new electronic resources and preparing them for the overall impact of computer technology is a normal consideration, and good tips for such training are published in the library literature. Sometimes, the cost of staff training can even be included in the purchase cost of the resource.

A sometimes hidden consideration is the cost of training the library patron. Many times this is one-on-one training that can take a large percentage of staff time. Many patrons will not immediately ask for help, and some will simply give up and walk away out of frustration.

Libraries can avoid this outcome by scheduling patron trainings when the resource is still relatively new. In a school or university library, the library staff can schedule classes into an orientation session. With a public or special library, free seminars on "Using Our New Electronic Resources" may be a cost-effective measure as well as a good public relations strategy.

At some point, patrons will begin teaching each other. This will happen in two ways. The training may be done overtly, where one patron, observing that another is looking around for help, offers friendly assistance, proud to show that he or she is competent. Training also sometimes happens covertly, as patrons eye others at the terminal and watch what they do. For this casual kind of training to happen, however, a fairly large percentage of the patron population must be comfortable with the technology, and even then there is no control over the quality of the training.

An electronic resources program is never finished. More resources are constantly being produced in electronic form. The choices are becoming more and more difficult, and the list of programs that a library will consider essential becomes more lengthy with each year. A consideration is the fact that only one patron can use a computer at one time; the average length of time that a complete patron search will take with a product is crucial to the choice. A program will not be cost-efficient if it becomes essentially a learning game occupying one patron for thirty minutes to an hour.

The good news is that if library staff members and patrons are well trained on one database product, they will quickly adapt to another product. All databases are searched in essentially the same way (see chapter 3), and once the staff is comfortable with several products, others are added with relative ease.

2

Hardware Requirements

An electronic resource program can consist of one computer in a library or a network with many hundreds of computers and access to a variety of sources. Most libraries will be somewhere in between these two extremes. Each library is different, and building an electronic information resources program must be considered in terms of the mission and goals of the institution.

There is no universal "right" choice for hardware or software with which to build the perfect electronic resource program. Each library needs to make the choices that are appropriate for their program and that fit within the parameters set by its parent institution.

With limited funds available, a library may elect to gradually acquire hardware for electronic information resources over a period of several years. If that tactic is chosen, it is wise to plan thoroughly and make sure that the hardware purchased will be viable over the long term and will be compatible with the resources that will eventually become part of the program.

Compatibility with electronic resource components is a key point in choosing hardware. Each electronic information product has specific requirements in terms of disk size, the kind of monitor, and even as minor a point as the speed of the modem. Before purchasing any piece of equipment, survey as many as possible of the electronic resource programs that are being considered for purchase. Ask specifically if a product will work on the equipment that you are buying. Pay particular attention to products that are new on the market, even if the resource is far beyond your budgeted price range. Many times new products arrive on the market at a high price and then become much more affordable in succeeding years. Be cautious with a preliminary equipment purchase—resources requiring different hardware may soon become available.

It is also a good idea to double-check the products you are buying for compatibility with the hardware. Ask the hardware vendor if there have been any compatibility problems with the electronic resource that you are intending to purchase.

An important point to consider in developing an electronic resources program is that the field is evolving at ever-increasing speed. Equipment purchases made today have to work with products that are being developed tomorrow. A "good deal" that will work with a specific product may well turn out to be totally useless in the future. It is far better to pass up a "sale item" and instead purchase equipment that is considered to be an industry standard. Choose companies that have been in existence for some years and that you assume will be in business for years to come.

Sometimes the term *workstation* is used to refer to a computer that is not networked, meaning not connected to any other computer. The term *stand-alone* also describes the computer workstation. The opposite of a stand-alone workstation is a *terminal*. A library may have one large computer holding the programs and databases and then use several terminals scattered throughout the library. The terminals are connected to the master computer and are dependent on that computer for programs and basic operational functions.

Some terminals consist of only a monitor and a keyboard, with all of their operating functions stored in the master computer. These are called *dumb terminals*. This is certainly the most inexpensive way to acquire terminals. However, a more versatile application is to use computers that could function very well as stand-alone workstations if necessary.

The descriptions used above are not standard. A library may proudly refer to six student "workstations" in the reference area that are more accurately defined as terminals. A new term beginning to be used is the *scholar's workstation*, which refers to computers providing access to a variety of information, whether or not the computer is networked.

For the purposes of this book, the terms *workstation* and *terminal* will be used interchangeably.

COMPONENTS
OF A WORKSTATION

Designing the ideal workstation for a specific library is rather like designing the ideal kitchen. Everyone needs a stove, sink, and refrigerator, of course, but the choices certainly do not end there. Considerations such as how much time you spend in the kitchen, whether or not you are a gourmet cook, and how much efficiency you need in your life are all important factors.

The same thing is true of designing a computer environment. A stand-alone workstation may be just a computer with a monitor and keyboard, or it may have any number of attachments (called *peripherals*). These may include a printer, modem, mouse, or other accessory. The workstation can be placed in a carrel shielding it from view or on a table alongside several other workstations. It can be connected to other workstations on a network or be set up as a stand-alone.

The basic configuration for a stand-alone workstation will be a computer with a hard drive, a color monitor, a printer, and, perhaps, a modem. If the computer is networked so that several computers are using the same CD-ROM or database, usually only one computer needs to have a hard drive. This can be a good choice, because computers without hard drives can be fairly inexpensive.

STANDARD PERIPHERALS
Modem: internal or external device that allows the user to communicate via telephone lines with other computers
Printer: makes "hard copy" (prints on paper)
Mouse: small hand-controlled device that allows the user to operate the computer without using the keyboard

Remember that you need not be a computer expert to make the right hardware choice; you just have to ask the right questions.

Big Blue or the Big Apple?

The first big choice that you will have to make is whether to go with IBM-compatible equipment or hardware from the Macintosh/Apple computer family. Just about every other choice you make will depend on what you choose for the basic computer. Generally speaking, most products work with an IBM-compatible computer; in the future, more products will probably work with the Macintosh family. Survey the information products that you are even remotely considering to see how much your hardware choice will limit your options.

It is a good idea to consider what computers your institution uses for other purposes. Training and installation will be less difficult, and it will be easier and faster to get repairs made, if you stay within the precedent set by your institution. Another advantage of using this approach is that computer equipment is constantly being upgraded. For many library applications, the fastest or most current upgrade is not always necessary. Sometimes workstations that have been replaced by upgrades at one location can be transferred for use at other locations in the organization.

Hard Drive

Most beginning electronic information resources programs require a computer that has a hard drive. There are very few electronic resources that do not require a hard drive, and even those that do not will work much faster if the hard drive is used.

A hard drive is an information storage disk located inside the computer. On this drive you will store hard-disk-resident databases, the software needed to run a CD-ROM program, and/or the telecommunications software needed for online searching. The size of the hard drive needed depends on the amount of software that is intended for purchase. Generally speaking, a 30- or 40-megabyte hard drive is more than sufficient to store most electronic resource program software, although a larger drive may be needed if the computer will be used as the base for a network.

Processor

The speed of a computer is also a consideration. Speed is even more of a consideration if the library plans to use one computer for a variety of uses. The amount of time that it takes a patron to exit one resource and begin using another may be several minutes on a slow computer. The part of a computer that controls the speed is called the processor.

When you see a product that seems fast or slow as it is being used by a vendor at a demonstration in your library or at a conference, ask about the speed of the processor in that computer. When equipment purchases are being considered, compare the processor under consideration with the vendor's processor. The higher the number, the faster the processor. In the world of IBM computers and their compatibles, a 486 processor is considerably faster than a 386.

A problem that occurs, albeit rarely, is that the library may be using an older version of software and then may buy a new computer that is too fast for the old software. Check with your hardware vendor to avoid this problem.

Monitor

The screen of a computer is called the monitor. A color monitor should be considered not a luxury but rather a necessity for an electronic resources program. Reasons often given for purchasing color monitors focus on attractiveness to users and other aesthetic considerations. A fact that may be easier to defend in a budget presentation is that some electronic resources now contain pictures that can only be seen on color monitors. In fact, some of these resources will not work at all unless a color monitor is attached.

Large-screen instruction is also possible with a color monitor. That is, the image on the computer screen can be projected onto a larger screen so that prospective users can see the product in action. This capability is extremely advantageous during training and orientation sessions, but it requires a computer with a color monitor.

SOME CONSIDERATIONS FOR PURCHASING HARDWARE
Size of the hard drive
Color or monochrome monitor
Will the programs require sound?
Is it capable of large-screen projection?

There are various kinds of color monitors available, including EGA, VGA, MCGA, and other types. Again, survey the field to determine the monitor that will work best with the widest variety of electronic products. It is far better to buy the latest kind of monitor available on the market than to buy an older version. Most of the products will soon require the newer monitor.

Sometimes budget considerations make it necessary to buy the more inexpensive monochrome monitors. If this is the decision, it would be wise to put color monitors on one or two computers and then buy monochrome for the remainder. That way, any use that requires a color monitor can be directed to those workstations.

Modem

A modem (modulator-demodulator) allows a computer to connect with another computer via a telephone line. Modems are essential for online searching and may also be needed for other purposes. The modem is a relatively inexpensive part of the computer, with some available for under $100.

Modems can be either internal or external. Internal modems are installed inside the computer, and external modems are connected to the computer by cables. About the only advantage of an external modem is that it will have some sort of blinking light to let the user know that it is working. This is a very minor consideration; unless the modem needs to be removed from the computer on a regular basis, an internal modem is generally preferable.

A modem is used for online searching, and the fee structure for the search will be based on the amount of time the user is online. A fast modem not only will save a user time, it will usually save the library money. Some information vendors charge customers different rates according to the speed of their modems. Rates are higher if a fast modem is used. If you have a fast modem, this could be an important selection criterion for an online information vendor.

The speed of a modem is measured in bits-per-second, or *Baud*. The Baud rate is usually measured in hundreds, but as the modems get faster and faster they will be measured in points. For instance, a 9600 Baud modem is also referred as a 9.6. A 9600 Baud modem is almost standard at this printing, but modems with speeds of 19.6 or even higher are becoming fairly common.

Printer

Electronic resources allow patrons to obtain information much faster and much more efficiently than print sources do. This efficiency is greatly reduced if patrons must use paper and pencil to copy down information from the computer screen. Not only will the patron lose efficiency, but it also will take much longer for each patron to complete his or her search. The cost-efficiency of electronic resources depends on the number of patrons using the resource. Attaching a printer to each workstation is one way to ensure that each patron completes a search quickly and then moves off, freeing the computer for another patron. For maximum efficiency, each computer station should have its own attached printer, although it is possible for two or more computers to share a printer.

There are problems inherent in using printers. Paper tends to get jammed or run out, ribbons must be replaced, and the printers themselves can be distractingly noisy. These problems are frustrating to the patrons and to library employees, who must frequently interrupt their work to come to the aid of a patron in mid-search. Even more frustrating is the patron who is too timid to tell the library staff that there is a problem and simply walks away to let the next patron deal with it.

Expect that a great deal of staff time will be spent in tending the printers. This time can be reduced by a careful choice of printers and quick, periodic inspection of the printer stations several times during the day. This inspection need only take a few seconds. It should consist of a glance for paper jams, which should be suspected if the paper appears to be crooked or wrinkled at the point where it enters the printer. The paper supply should be checked to make sure that there is sufficient quantity for the next several patrons. Finally, the online button (sometimes called the *select* button) should be checked to make sure that it is on.

This last problem is particularly vexing, especially because it is so easy to fix. Each printer has a green light to indicate that it is ready to receive information from the computer. This is called being "on line," and there is usually a button that takes the printer on and off line. In order to remove paper from the printer and automatically feed a fresh sheet of paper in, the printer must be momentarily taken off line. The online button needs to be pressed again to place the printer back on line. If a patron walks away with a printout and forgets to press the online button, the printer will not work for the next patron unless he or she presses the button.

Library staff should be trained that each time they walk near a printer they should glance at it quickly to check for jams and paper supply and to make sure the online button is on. It will add very few seconds to their work but will save them much aggravation. New ribbons and computer paper should be stored in a convenient place, along with long tweezers for removing bits of paper from jams. Other tips for using printers include providing patrons with clear directions for removing the printout and for troubleshooting. If the printers are used a great deal, it is possible to position the entire box of paper underneath the printer table so that the library staff is not constantly installing paper in the printers.

There are a variety of printers available in a variety of price ranges. At the very top of the price range are color printers. These are valuable in printing charts and graphs, but this limited use will not justify the purchase unless the library has many computer stations and can designate one for use with a color printer.

Laser printers are also quite expensive. A laser printer is similar to a high-quality copier, and the quality of laser-printed pages is very much like that of a high-quality copy. Laser printers do not use ribbons; they use toner, just like a copier. They are also almost silent when printing, which is a definite advantage in a library setting. If laser printers are seen as desirable but are out of the library's price range, it is possible to purchase one laser printer and have each computer networked to it so that patrons can use the computer at one location, then go to another area in the library to pick up their copies. If this area is not staffed, there is a potential problem with patrons sorting out which copies are theirs, especially during busy times. However, if the library is charging patrons a per-page fee for printing information, it would be easy to install the printer near or behind the reference desk, so that patrons would pay for copies as they retrieve them.

The simplest solution, and the one that most libraries will choose, is to place an inexpensive printer beside each computer. A printer can be purchased very cheaply, and because much of the printouts that patrons make are disposable, the quality of the printing is not really a factor.

Most printers are of the *dot-matrix* type, meaning that the individual letters are made up of dots. The quality of the printer is measured in dots per inch (pins). A 24-pin printer is of fairly high quality. A 9-pin printer would be of lower quality but would probably be much faster. Some printers have a variety of settings that allow patrons to choose the size of the type and the quality of the printout. This may or may not be a positive consideration; patrons are likely to change settings to fit their needs and then neglect to change the settings back to standard for the next patron.

The two characteristics that are of most concern in printer selection are the amount of noise that the printer makes and the number of routine problems (such as paper jams) that the library staff has to fix. If printers are being added to existing workstations, it may be a good idea to ask a vendor for a sample printer to see how many times the library staff must be engaged with printer problems.

The noise problem can be alleviated with plastic boxes that go over the printer to reduce the noise, but these are rather bulky. It may be simpler to make quietness one of the criteria for purchase.

When you are shopping for a printer, the vendor will be happy to demonstrate the many features of the printer. It may print letters double-wide or double-high and do other fairly useless tricks. Instead of focusing on the glitzy features, ask the vendor to demonstrate how to add paper to the printer, then assess how easy it will be for a typical library patron to follow those instructions. Ask the vendor to demonstrate how to clear a paper jam and make a judgment as to whether or not this can be done by patrons. With both of the above, be sure to ask the vendor how doing the operation wrong could damage the printer. Some printers are extremely delicate, whereas others can take a fair amount of abuse and still continue to function.

Try to purchase the same make and model of printer for most or all of the workstations in the library. Not only will the library save money in buying ribbons and other supplies, but if some printers must be out for repair or become unusable during a busy time in the library, printers can be shifted from one computer to another with little trouble. It also means that library staff will become fairly expert at configuring the printer and at using the special features.

CONSIDERATIONS FOR CHOOSING A PRINTER
Paper is easy to load
Minimum of problems such as paper jams
Quiet
Easy-to-read controls on front of printer

Furthermore, at some point in the process of adding electronic software programs, the installation procedure will ask what printer is being used. If different printers are being used at each station, this may cause some problems if printers are moved around.

In spite of the problems with printers, it is important for an electronic information program to allow patrons to print information that they find on the computer. It is not cost-efficient for a patron to have almost instantaneous access to information but then have to stand in front of the screen copying down information with paper and pencil while other patrons are waiting their turn.

CD-ROM Drive

The CD-ROM drive is usually an external component of the computer system, but some CD-ROM drives are now installed directly. If space is a problem on the computer table, the CD-ROM player need not be placed beside the computer; it can be placed on the processor, with the monitor on top of the CD-ROM drive. This arrangement will take up much less room on the table and give the patron more room for books and papers.

Compatibility can be a problem with the CD-ROM drive. Nothing is more frustrating than purchasing a CD-ROM resource and finding it will not work with the CD-ROM drive that the library owns. Ask the CD-ROM software vendors three questions: what CD-ROM drive they would recommend purchasing to use with the product; what other CD-ROM drives work with the product; and what drives will not work with the product.

The first and second questions above apply to different situations. Most CD-ROM products can be purchased with their own workstations. This is an option for the library if the budget for equipment is restricted, and the software purchased could include its own hardware. The CD drive that the software vendor recommends purchasing will most likely be the one that is sold with the product. However, the second question lets the prospective buyer see what other options are available. The answers to those questions from a variety of CD-ROM vendors should produce a relatively trustworthy list of CD-ROM drives and give some idea of what CD-ROM drives work with most of the products available.

If the library program has more CD-ROM products than computers, it is possible to place all of the software needed to run the individual CD products on the hard drive of the computer and then switch the CDs in the player as needed. The library staff will have to consider whether to allow patrons to insert and remove CDs from the drive or require the patron to ask for staff assistance. If theft is a problem, it might be wise to consider a CD drive that can be locked so that the CD inside cannot be removed.

Other Hardware
Considerations

Pieces of computer equipment are connected to each other by cables. A complete computer workstation will have a mass of cables behind it linking all of the separate pieces. In a computer area with several computers sharing a table, it will be impossible to separate the cables that belong to each computer. There are peripherals that help to manage cabling. At the very least, the cables belonging to each computer can be physically tied together for the appearance of neatness.

Also, every piece of computer equipment must be plugged into an electrical outlet. Libraries that are being renovated to include electronic resources need an adequate number of outlets. The easiest way for librarians to make sure that they have adequately planned for enough electrical outlets is to use the strip outlets that have the sockets every few inches. Even though this may seem like a tremendous number of outlets, they will all be used before much time has passed. Experienced electronic resource users know that, along with too rich or too thin, a library can not have too many electrical outlets.

Some strips come with power surge protectors to prevent a surge of electricity from damaging the computers. If the electrical supply to the library is inconsistent or the library is in an area that is subject to frequent thunderstorms, this precaution may be a necessity.

If online searching is planned, a telephone line is essential. The best arrangement by far is to have a dedicated telephone line, although doing so is expensive. A dedicated telephone line has its own number; it is not an extension of any other number and does not go through a switchboard. A dedicated line will result in far fewer problems with online searching because it will decrease static.

It is possible for a library to use a voice telephone line for online searching. That option will work as long as the telephone users know when a search is in progress. Otherwise, the online connection will be interrupted when someone lifts the telephone receiver.

If installing a new telephone line is impossible, it may still be possible for the library to offer online searching. If the librarian can make a telephone call without talking to a switchboard operator or can reach an outside line by dialing "9" or another special number, then online searching may be possible, although there may be some problems with static or interrupted searches.

Other cost-effective measures are to install one telephone line and have several computers share the line. When one computer begins using the line, the others will be unable to use it; however, if a user at another computer does not know that the line is being used and starts to dial the modem, it may disrupt the first connection. A better way to do this kind of sharing is with an "A/B switch." This connection is a small box that rests between the computers. When the arrow on the box is turned to "A," computer "A" has the telephone line; when it is turned to "B," computer "B" has the connection. A/B switches can also be used to share printers between computers.

The A/B switch in an inexpensive method to use when the electronic information program is in the early stages. If the computers are networked, a network modem can be added to give multiple users access to online resources. The level of security needed for any specific library may partly determine the degree of independence a library patron has when using online resources.

If the library is considering adding a fax machine to the electronic resources program, this can be placed on the same telephone line as the computer modem. It is of course ideal for each piece of equipment to have its own telephone line, but in some cases it may be necessary to start small and add additional pieces to the program later.

Remember that a fax machine can both initiate and receive telephone calls. With online searching, the computer almost always initiates the call and rarely receives them. Therefore, the fax machine can be set up to answer on the first ring. When the phone rings, it will be a fax; the fax machine will answer and receive the call. When the electronic resources program gets more mature and becomes busier, it will be a problem for a fax machine to share a telephone line with online searching equipment, but for the first year or two it could be a workable solution if resources are limited.

FURNITURE

There are as many varieties of computer furniture as there are computers; in fact, there may be more. Wheeled carts, padded carrels, and plain tables are just a few of the variety of options available. The best advice is to purchase the furnishings that have the most flexibility and are in line with the library decor.

Using existing furniture is certainly an option, although doing so may cause a few minor problems. Most computer furniture has electrical outlets on the table within easy access. Most library reference tables do not. Moreover, some library reference tables have a raised edge toward the back. Although this edge does prevent books and papers from sliding off the table, it also is a problem for computer cables: The height at which the computer cable plugs into the machine is sometimes below the height of the raised edge. If the cable is extremely stiff, it may be damaged if it is bent back over the edge. At the very least, the computer will have to be pulled further out onto the table, which will give the patron less work room.

"Modesty panels," which sit underneath the tables to provide a screen to facing occupants, are also a problem for computer cables. At some point, someone will have to crawl underneath the table to remove or untangle cables. The panels make it impossible to reach the back of the computer, and removing them sometimes makes the table wobbly.

Flat computer tables probably offer the greatest flexibility. These have an adequate work area, can be moved around with ease, and, although certainly not designed to win architectural awards, are functional pieces. A computer workstation, complete with CD-ROM player and printer, will take as much as four feet of table space.

A major decision for the library program may be whether to have patrons stand or sit at computer terminals. Patrons generally take less time to do a search at standing terminals, so that may be a consideration in a busy library. The higher tables also make the computers more visible to patrons as they walk into the library. This increased visibility also makes it easier for the library staff to supervise the workstation from across the room.

It is a good idea to have at least one "sitting" terminal, and it should be at a table that can accommodate a wheelchair-bound patron.

QUESTIONS TO ASK

In the world of *computerese*, there are many problems that an unsuspecting librarian may run into that have not even been dreamed of. This section will not solve these problems, but it will give you some fodder for discussion with the computer expert at your institution.

Slots

The first look inside the computer is a surprise to many novice computer users. The best way to describe it is to say that it looks like the view of a city from an airplane. It mainly consists of circuit boards and other electronic mazes, all interconnected by wires. If you are a novice user, ask to see inside the computer; this will help you visualize problems that may occur.

A computer has extra places, called *slots*, for the extra pieces of equipment that a user wishes to add. Each piece that gets attached to the computer, such as a printer or a modem, needs the appropriate card in a slot inside the computer. If the computer is being placed on a network, a network card must be placed in a slot.

The number of slots that the computer has is not endless, and it may be possible to run out of slots. An inexpensive, basic computer may not be the best deal in the long run. Peripherals that could easily be required by an electronic resource include a mouse, color monitor, printer, CD drive, or modem. Each of these may take a slot inside the computer. Ask when buying the computer how many empty slots it has.

There are ways to get around the problem of slots. For example, sometimes more than one function can be placed on a card. Generally, if you are buying a computer with all of the accompaniments at one time, it will not be a problem. The problem arises when pieces are added to an existing computer system.

With an electronic resources program, there is always something to spend money on. These items can be as expensive as new reference tables or as inexpensive as mouse pads. Certainly, there will be a steady request for various accoutrements. Although the constant additions can get costly, they may save some money in the long run, because some of the purchases will add to the life of the computers.

Anti-static pads are such a device. When patrons walk across a carpeted area to the computer, they may build up a static electricity charge. When they touch the computer, a small spark of static electricity may occur. Although seemingly a minor point, that small spark could damage your computer. Computers are electronic devices. They do not handle sparks of electricity well. At the very least, the static may cause problems with how well and how fast networked CDs operate. Anti-static pads fit under the computer and ground the electric charge. If the library has a problem with dryness, these pads should be considered as an initial purchase.

The mouse that attaches to the computer works either by the rolling of a small ball inside the mouse or via a sensor as the mouse is drawn across a special pad. Either way, there are special mouse pads that prevent the mouse or the table from becoming scratched. If the resources that you are purchasing require a mouse, you might consider this purchase.

Earlier, mention was made of large-screen projections. This allows whatever is being shown on the computer monitor to be projected onto a screen, similar to how a projector shows a movie. The user can control the computer keyboard exactly as if using the monitor, and the computer will react to the commands as usual. This can be an extremely useful tool for training, because the trainees can be taken step by step through the search process. Alternate ways to do a particular step can be demonstrated in front of the group, and questions the group raises can be answered visually instead of just verbally.

There are several ways to do large-screen viewing. One possibility is to use one or two 25- to 27-inch television monitors and place them on tall carts so that the audience can see the television screens. This set-up has distinct advantages if the quality of picture is of importance. The image will be as bright and clear as it was on the computer screen, if not more so. However, this will not work with all television monitors. In order to figure out how to make it work in your situation, you may have to check back and forth between the computer experts and the television experts, perhaps several times.

Another advantage of this method is that it can be used in a well-lighted room, as opposed to the other methods, which require some dimming of the lights.

A totally separate possibility is to use a projection panel. This device fits on top of a regular overhead projector and projects onto a screen the image that would be shown on the computer monitor. Some manufacturers have combined the computer and overhead technology and are offering data projectors. The projectors are available in a variety of quality levels, including full color. Compatibility is sometimes an issue with this equipment; you may want to test several models before making a decision.

Be sure also to test using a variety of electronic products. Sometimes a highlighted or bold-printed word on a computer screen will show up as a blank on the projected image, which can be confusing to potential users during a demonstration.

A video projector, similar to those that can project the image from a VCR onto a large screen, can also be used to project a data image. These have not been on the market long but will soon be dropping in price enough to be on the shelves of every institution.

Choosing the correct hardware is not easy. It requires an expenditure of time in looking at the various choices and a readiness to ask questions when any point is not understood. It is better to appear dense than to make a poor choice of equipment that you will have to live with. Unless an institution has on-site computer repair technicians, the library staff will have to handle minor emergencies themselves. It is best to choose the equipment that you will be most comfortable with.

QUICK CHECK OF ELECTRONIC RESOURCES AREA

1. Printers:
   - Online buttons lit?
   - Any paper jams?
   - Enough paper?

2. Are the computer screens at the main menu ready for the next patron?

3. Is the area free from litter, excess paper, and so on?

4. If patrons are at terminals, do they need assistance?

Performing this simple checklist on a regular basis will help keep staff interruptions to a minimum.

3

General
Criteria

In some ways, the selection process for an electronic resource is much the same as the selection process for any other library resource. The same criteria of authoritativeness, accuracy of content, and appropriateness in the collection still apply to the selection of these resources. Librarians making the choice for electronic sources can begin with these same criteria in mind.

However, the nature of electronic resources brings additional criteria to the selection process. These additional criteria include format, hardware requirements, advances in technology, and ease of use. Making a purchase decision on electronic resources involves careful consideration of the effect that electronic searching has on the effectiveness of the product. The searching capability and cost of each format must be factored in.

There are many similarities in the ways databases are organized and searched. These similarities are a great aid to the librarian, because once patrons and library staff learn how to use one electronic product, others can be added with little disruption. With very minor variations, the same kinds of searches can be done in all products. The commands to do these searches may differ widely, but once users understand how the product works, the commands are learned without much of a problem. This universal set of searching techniques is called *database theory*. When considering purchase of an electronic resource for a library program, these general criteria should be considered essential for the product.

Think of purchases of database products in terms of cost-effectiveness. The faster staff and patrons learn to use the product, the greater the number of patrons that can perform searches in a set period of time, adding to the cost-effectiveness of the resource.

Products that do not take full advantage of the searching options offered by the electronic format are not cost-effective. Products that have extraneous features are not cost-effective either; although some patrons may view the features as interesting or even necessary, the increase in the amount of time that it takes those patrons to use the material will greatly decrease the cost-effectiveness of the product.

This chapter presents a discussion of features common to all electronic resources.

ORGANIZATION AND INDEXING

As discussed in chapter 1, a database is a pile of information that is separated into fields for searching. When searching for information, the patron must use the software to give the computer instructions; electronic databases cannot think (although there are those who claim that day is not far off). A computer does not know what the user is looking for, and it does not know the concept of words; it merely searches for an exact match of the keystrokes, including spaces, entered by a user. It only knows to look in the places it was programmed to look or in the places specified by the user.

Browse Mode

There are in general two main ways to search any electronic database. It is important for all electronic database products to offer both modes of searching. The first is to browse through an alphabetical list of all the indexed words contained in a specific field. In a magazine index, for example, the user could browse through an alphabetic list of all of the words contained in the subject field. In an encyclopedia, the most commonly browsed field is usually the title field.

When searching in the browse mode, the user types in a word or phrase that closely matches his or her search topic. The computer matches up the word with the alphabetic subject or title list and finds those that most closely match the word(s) input by the user. The screen would show a list of words or phrases, with the closest match indicated by a highlighted bar or blinking cursor square. The user can then page up or down to get closer to the intended topic. It is helpful to know what field is being searched in the browse mode; the patron may choose different words depending on whether the subject field or the title field is being searched.

Sometimes the user can choose from among several fields in the browse mode, but this is rare. For example, there is a product that offers either Library of Congress or Sears subject headings (see fig. 3.1) Usually, the only field that can be searched in the electronic version of a source is the same field that can be searched in the print version.

Teaching the browse mode is a good first step in training, because prospective users can visualize turning the pages of an encyclopedia or looking up subject headings in a magazine index. The only difference is that the article titles or subject headings are in a list format. In addition, the browse mode is excellent for simple searches with general topics. A good rule of thumb is that if the subject of the search can be described in one word, the browse method will most likely be effective. It can also be helpful if the user wants a few citations that will be used for the very beginning of research or for very general information.

```
Z_____N
] [[[[[   [[          [[[[[  Social    ^
] [[           \\     [[     Issues    ^      Z_____N
] [[[[[   [[  [[[[]  [[[[[  Resources ^      ] Release #  ^
]    [[   [[   [[      [[    Series,   ^      ]     3.16    ^
] [[[[[   [[   [[    [[[[[  Inc.      ^      @VVVVVVVVVVVVY
@VVVVVVVVVVVVVVVVVVVVVVVVVVVVVVVVVVVVVVY

                        M E N U
]                                              ^
]   A. Library of Congress Subject Headings    ^
]   B. Title Browse (List by SIRS Volume/Year) ^
]   C. Keyword Search                          ^
CDDDDDDDDDDDDDDDDDDDDDDDDDDDDDDDDDDDDDDDDDDDDDDDX
]   D. Quit                                     ^
@VVVVVVVVVVVVVVVVVVVVVVVVVVVVVVVVVVVVVVVVVVVVVVVY


F1 - Help         <Enter> to Select        (c) 1992 SIRS, Inc.
```

Fig. 3.1. Library of Congress Subject Headings Search on SIRS System. Reprinted by permission.

However, the user cannot always determine the field that will be browse-searched. Usually that field is preset by the producer. For example, if a user wanted to browse through a list of authors in a magazine index database, that option may not be available. The producer will also make decisions as to what words are used as subjects or titles. "Drunk Driving" may seem to be a logical choice for a subject heading on this popular topic for high school compositions, but the term used by the producer may be "Automobile drivers—Alcohol use."

In the browse mode, users must type in a one-word topic or the first word in a phrase. Typing in "foreign relations," when that is in fact a subheading of other subjects, may be misleading. The product should offer some type of *see* or *see also* references for unsuccessful searches; most patrons will not know what to do next unless it is clearly indicated.

Users have to learn through experience or training that when searching in browse mode, finding no "hits" does not mean that the subject is not in the source; it may mean simply that particular subject cannot be located through the browse mode. In order to search other fields, another mode of searching must be used.

Word Search Mode

The other mode of searching is called by various terms, including *word search* and *keyword;* in this book it will be referred to as *word search*. In this mode, the computer searches across multiple fields for a word or string of words that the user inputs (see fig. 3.2, p. 28).

```
 <ENTER> to Select                                      <ESC> to go back
Z_____N
]                         Keyword Search                                ^
CDDDDDDDDDDDDDDDDDDDDDDDDDDDDDDDDDDDDDDDDDDDDDDDDDDDDDDDDDDDDDDDDDDDDDDDDDDX
]                                      Within    Same         Total      ^
]                    Words             # words   Order      Articles     ^
]                                                                        ^
]         SUPREME COURT                  1        Yes          434       ^
]                                                                        ^
]    And...WOMEN                                              1701       ^
]                                                                        ^
]    And...                                                              ^
]    B                                                                   ^
]                                                           Total        ^
] Press <A> for And, <O> for Or, <N> for Not                            ^
@VVVVVVVVVVVVVVVVVVVVVVVVVVVVVVVVVVVVVVVVVVVVVVVVVVVVVVVVVVVVVVVVVVVVVVVVVY


     Z_____N
     ] Irregular plural :WOMAN                      Total   1240  ^
     ] Would you like to include plural?  [Y]es  or  [N]o        ^
     @VVVVVVVVVVVVVVVVVVVVVVVVVVVVVVVVVVVVVVVVVVVVVVVVVVVVVVVVVVVVVY

 F1 - Help                                              F9 - Menu
```

Fig. 3.2. Word Search in SIRS System. Reprinted by permission.

Precision is essential in word search mode. The computer will either find a word that matches the input word exactly, keystroke for keystroke, or it will find nothing. Hitting the space bar on the computer is counted as a keystroke. If the words are not in the database exactly as the user inputs them, the computer responds with a message informing the user that the search has been unsuccessful. With a simple search of one or two words, the user should find at least some information. Finding no hits is more likely an indication that the search was conducted incorrectly than that the database contains no information on that subject.

Not all fields are searched in the word search mode. Somewhere in the accompanying documentation or manual there should be a list of exactly which fields are searched in this mode. In a magazine index, the fields most commonly searched in this mode are subject, title, and author. In an encyclopedia, the user might search article title, text, and perhaps even bibliography.

Some fields cannot be searched. In a magazine index, for example, it is fairly common to search for articles on a particular subject in a particular magazine. However, the user cannot search for all articles under five pages. Similarly, it is not possible to search the bibliography in an encyclopedia for all books published by a certain publisher. Granted, very few patrons will need or even want to attempt this kind of search; these examples are given simply to emphasize that electronic resources cannot answer every single reference question that may arise.

Each database product will offer one mode as the primary search mode and the other as a secondary mode. Imagine that you are a library patron standing at the computer for the very first time. If you do not know what choice to make, you would probably simply hit the enter key. Whatever search mode begins naturally when patrons hit the enter key is the primary method of searching for that product.

In a magazine index, the browse function is usually the primary search mode. In most encyclopedias, it is the word search mode. Because most patrons, especially inexperienced ones, will just hit the enter key in lieu of another choice, the primary mode will be the one used most often in a library. Consider the effectiveness of that search mode for the routine information requests that patrons have in your library.

One way to judge a product is to think of several routine information requests for which library patrons might use it. In exhibit halls, some vendors like to ask librarians on the prowl to pick a difficult search. However, it is probably better to stay with routine searches to evaluate an electronic product. All librarians have that one request that stays with them because the information could not be located in the library or because the search topic was unique and intriguing. It is questionable if it is wise to spend several thousand dollars to solve that one unique search problem. It is better to buy a product that will aid the majority of patrons in their more routine searches.

The browse mode is the easiest for patrons to use and can in fact probably be used by most patrons without any training. It is limiting, however, because patrons must know the subject or title for which they are searching. A good product will expand the use of this mode by offering *see* and *see also* references, but it would be interesting to measure exactly how many patrons actually use these references.

The word search mode is more complicated for patrons, and most will likely require more training, both to learn how to use this mode at all and to learn to use the expanded capabilities of this mode. Some inexperienced patrons will run searches that come up with zero hits (meaning that no information could be found on that topic) when in fact they either misspelled a word, contained too many words in their search topic, or otherwise overcomplicated their search.

Boolean Searching

One of the benefits of the word search mode is that it offers the possibilities of expert searching techniques. In this context, the word *expert* refers not to an extreme talent in searching but rather to the use of more sophisticated search techniques. A librarian, even one with very limited computer ability, will very quickly become comfortable with expert techniques.

One of the more powerful techniques is *Boolean searching*. The Boolean searching theory is taken directly from ninth-grade Algebra I class, which all librarians at one time took—and passed. (The fact that, after years of putting it behind us, math comes back to haunt us is one of the sad facts of working as an information professional in the 1990s.)

Boolean searching uses the operators of *and*, *or*, and *not* to combine words (see fig. 3.3, p. 30). Suppose a user wishes to conduct a search for information on teenage drug and alcohol use. This would be a difficult or even impossible search in the browse mode because it is unlikely that the user would chance on the exact subject heading—even if one subject heading that covered this topic existed. The user would have to pick through all of the hits found on the topic of drug abuse and pick out those citations dealing with teenagers, then do the same for alcoholism.

AND

OR

NOT

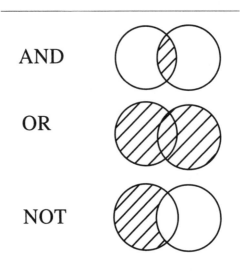

Fig. 3.3. Boolean Operators

With Boolean searching, however, the user can search for "teen or teenage or youth or adolescent" and combine that with a search for "drug or alcohol." Some databases even allow the user to specify that the search words be so many words apart in the text or in the same field or paragraph.

The use of the Boolean operator *not* is generally not encouraged in the searching world. Like life, electronic search techniques are always more productive when worded positively rather than negatively. The best use for the *not* operand is in a search for a phrase that has two distinctly different contexts. For instance, suppose a user wanted to find information about Martin Luther. If the user just searched for the words "Martin" and "Luther," certainly some of the information found would be about Martin Luther. However, at least part and probably the majority of the hits found would be about Martin Luther King. The search would be best done by asking for the words Martin and Luther, and *not* King. Remember, though, that if there were any articles about Martin Luther interacting with a king, this information would be eliminated also.

When using electronic resources, it is best not to think of searching for subjects or topics. A user is searching for *words*—more accurately, for a series of keystrokes. In our people profession, we are used to dealing with humans who will understand what we mean rather than what we say. That is not true of computers. The true skill in information retrieval is in choosing the words that best fit the subject or topic.

Truncation

Another expert searching technique is *truncation*, or the use of wild-card operators. The user can type in part of a word and then use a symbol that would allow the computer to search for all words beginning with the letters typed in. The symbols used in products vary widely. Truncation symbols used in some of the more common electronic products include *, #, @, $, :, and ?. The * symbol seems to be the standard truncation key in some of the newer products.

Using truncation allows the user to account for plurals, alternate spellings, and alternative forms of the same word. For instance, in the above search for information on teenage alcohol and drug use, truncation would allow the user to simplify the search to include fewer terms. Using the truncation symbol * along with Boolean searching, the search would look like this: "(teen* or youth or adolescent*) and (drug* or alcohol*)." This search would be very complete and would find most pertinent citations. Truncation can also be used with numbers (see fig. 3.4).

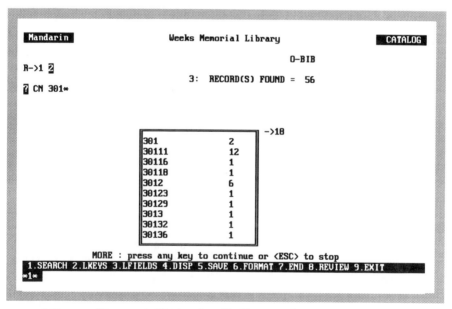

15   Expert Search; Call number 301

Fig. 3.4. Truncation of a Call Number. Reprinted by permission of Mandarin/ Mediaflex.

The danger of truncation is that some words have a variety of endings. It is much better to search for "cat" or "cats" than to use a truncation symbol—cat*. The latter search, in addition to yielding the desired information, would also give results for "catch" and "catheter" and "Catalina." The more words that a computer could possibly find, the longer the search will take. As in the above example, truncation does not always mean a more exact search. Sometimes it will broaden the search to the point of being meaningless. Try using a dictionary to see how many words could possibly start with the letters you are considering using.

Truncation will rarely be needed with one-word searches or searches for general information. If a patron wants information on libraries, a search for that one word will probably find more than enough information. However, if the search is for a topic such as a children's story hour in public libraries, then conceivably the truncated "librar*" could be used effectively.

Truncation is not used in the browse mode, although some patrons will incorrectly use it when typing in their search topic. Because the computer puts the user as close as possible to his or her search word, using truncation will not interfere with the success of the search, but it is simply unnecessary.

DOCUMENTATION

The most frustrating part of using an electronic resource is using the accompanying guide, called *documentation*, that accompanies the product. Documentation may contain installation instructions, but it mainly consists of instructions on the use of the product. Documentation for electronic products may vary in size from a few fold-out charts to a 300-page manual. The index is usually another source of frustration. Very rarely do the skills required to develop an excellent electronic product carry over to development of an excellent index to the use of that product. The documentation is either oversimplified, written in a breezy magazine style that gives little pertinent information, or too technical, so that the user does not understand the terminology used to describe the commands.

The most common complaint heard about documentation is that in order to look up the proper command with which to conduct a search, the user must *already know the command*. And if one knows the command already, why is there a need to look it up?

Always request to see the documentation before buying an electronic product. It is doubtful that a selection decision will rest solely on the quality of documentation, because patrons will rarely use the documentation and the library staff will only use it in the first few months the product is used. However, evaluating the quality of the documentation does give an indication of the ease with which the library staff will be able to quickly look up commands and the amount of time that will be spent learning the product. This translates into dollars of staff time, which is always a consideration.

When evaluating the documentation, look up several terms that were discussed earlier in the chapter, such as truncation or Boolean searching. In a quick five-minute read, decide how easy it is to determine what the browse and word search modes of searching are called, what the primary mode of searching is, what fields are searched in the word search mode, and other such items.

The documentation should include a quick-reference guide. This is an easy-to-read list of the product's common commands. This guide can be a laminated card or even a poster, and is very helpful when posted beside the product. If this guide is well written and concise, simply having it within the sight of the patron will solve the great majority of problems.

When a library installs its first electronic product, everyone who will come in contact with it will probably read the documentation cover to cover. With the next few products, documentation will be skimmed by a decreasing number of the library staff. Soon, new product documentation will simply be glanced at and placed on a shelf.

Second only to the frustration of improperly indexed documentation is the frustration of not being able to find the documentation when a problem occurs. Generally, when the documentation is needed, it is because there is a patron waiting at a terminal, which means, essentially, that there is down time when the product is not being used. It helps greatly if one shelf in a library is earmarked for the documentation for the electronic resources.

If there are several members of the library staff who will be assisting patrons with the product, the purchase of multiple copies of documentation should be considered. An idea might be to place one copy of the documentation near the product for patron use and another elsewhere for librarian use only.

REVIEW OF GENERAL SELECTION CRITERIA

Electronic resources are something of an educational bandwagon. Every library wants at least one and probably more, and every supplier of library materials is rushing to prepare some of these materials in electronic format. Some products are excellent research tools; some are excellent educational games; and some are simply print products transferred to electronic format, with no change in search capability or access.

Economic times are simply too tough for libraries to spend money on products that do not add value to the library program. That is true of $29.95 library books, and it is certainly true of $3,000 computer systems. Consider the following factors when you are preparing to purchase electronic information resource materials.

Format

Many of the products currently on the market are available in both print and electronic form, so when making purchase decisions, first consider whether the electronic format is the best choice. Some resources need only be purchased in the electronic form, some are most useful in the print format, and some should be held in both print and electronic formats.

Librarians weighing this decision must consider the content of the material. Just because a source is in electronic form, it is not automatically better than the same or a similar product in print form. If the library already has this source in the print form, investigate how much is it used. Visualize how the use would improve if the resource was in electronic form. Ask, "If this book were on a computer, how else would I want to look things up?"

Electronic sources can offer a variety of forms of access to content. The question is how significantly electronic searching improves the access over the print product. What can you do with the computer version that you cannot do with the print version? The next question is how many of your patrons will take advantage of that new and improved searching option.

A parallel can be drawn to the questions used in the initial integration of audio-visual materials in teaching. A guideline used in deciding whether or not to use audio-visual materials was whether the material could not be taught any other way. In order to be deemed useful, the audio-visual product had to be the best, perhaps even the *only,* way to illustrate an educational concept.

The same rule of thumb can be applied to the selection of electronic resources. Is the electronic search one that cannot be conducted in the print source? If not, is the search faster or more thorough than in the print source? If the print source and the electronic source are essentially the same, then purchase of the electronic source is questionable. For electronic resources to be cost-efficient, the search must be faster, more thorough, or more accessible than in the print format.

Word Searching

Another test is to consider whether the access that is provided in the electronic source significantly improves the access to the material. An example of this is the word search capability provided by many resources. Suppose a patron knows part of the title of a book or article, or remembers a certain word in it. That would be a difficult search in a print source. In an electronic source, however, this search is quite simple, because a product that offers word searching essentially indexes almost every word in that field.

Purchase Versus Lease

The cost of the print source versus the electronic source is another factor. The electronic source is not always more expensive in the long run. Some products can be annually updated for a greatly reduced fee. In the case of encyclopedias, this fee is less than $200. So if the library usually buys new sets of printed encyclopedias each year, it would actually be less expensive to purchase an electronic version.

Generally, purchasing electronic resources means the library can spend less money on print sources. However, once a CD-ROM magazine index has been implemented, fewer and fewer patron will use the print version anyway. It will not take many years before the librarian will consider dropping the print version, simply because of lack of use.

Before you make a decision to purchase a resource in electronic format, consider whether to buy or lease the product. The leasing of materials is not common with any type of resource except electronic resources. In leasing, the library pays a sum to the company to use its product. The library must agree to purchase each update of the product or return the original disk. This is a practice unheard of to most librarians. With print sources that are produced annually, libraries often purchase an updated volume only once every three or four years. Imagine a company telling a librarian that if the annual yearbook is not purchased each year, the entire set of encyclopedias must be returned!

Discuss with the vendor any problems you foresee with leasing. Sometimes library budgets may fluctuate wildly from one year to the next, especially with school districts in states where the public may vote on the budget. Suppose you buy a product that is well received in the library and used continually by patrons. The next year it is found that purchasing the update is impossible. With some products, you will have to return the original unless other arrangements are made with the company.

Authoritativeness

Even if the access to a product is improved in electronic form, the product itself does not automatically become better. Carefully read the reviews of the print source to check authoritativeness, accuracy of content, quality of indexing, and other factors. Any errors in the work may be magnified by being put into electronic form. If the resource does not exist in print form, check to make sure there is an authoritative source of information for the product and that the product is accurate and generally free from errors.

Readability

Even electronic products must still be read, and reading from a computer screen can be difficult for some patrons. The vendor should know the reading level of the product and the approximate age or grade level of its intended audience. The typeface should be large enough to read easily, and the screen should be free from the clutter of extraneous graphics or company logos.

Some products have a command line at the top or the bottom of the screen or picture icons giving additional search options to the patron. The command line or icons should be separated by enough space from the text so that the patron does not become confused and think that the command options shown are part of the text on the screen.

Searching Capability

All electronic products are searched in essentially the same ways. A database has certain fields, discussed in chapter 1 of this book, that can be searched. It is important when buying electronic resources to ensure that the maximum access to the content is attained. Think of the content of the product and decide what fields that patron would most likely want to search. The more fields that are indexed, the greater the flexibility of the product.

Boolean searching and word searching are an absolute necessity. It is hard to imagine a product that would not need Boolean search capability to provide maximum access to the content of the material. Without word searching, it is difficult to see what advantage the electronic source could provide over a print index.

Normal Versus Expert Mode

Most products have a general search mode that is easy for a beginning user or for a simple search, and a more advanced mode that involves more sophisticated searching techniques. It is amazing how quickly patrons become skilled on the expert mode. The directions for getting from one mode to the other should be given onscreen and be easy to follow.

These general criteria are ones that all electronic resources share. The next chapter covers the actual search process. Before you begin this part of the selection process, it might be wise to look at some of the products in action to review the criteria covered in this chapter.

GENERAL SELECTION CRITERIA

Format: Should this resource be purchased in print or electronic form?

Keyword Searching: Will the computer find the search word anywhere in the field, or must the search word be the first word in the field?

Purchase vs. Lease: Will the library own the product, or must an update or annual fee be included in each year's budget?

Authoritativeness: Is the source of information accurate and reliable?

Readability: What is the reading level of information, and how easy is the screen to read?

Searching Capability: Is Boolean searching included? What fields are indexed?

Normal vs. Expert Mode: Does the product have an expert mode for more advanced searching?

4

Getting Started

Moving a library program from having only print sources to offering both print and electronic resources is a long and involved process and should be carefully planned. Taking that first step out into the unknown world of electronic information can be scary. Fortunately, enough libraries of all types and sizes have gone through the process so that it is not necessary for each library program to make the same mistakes its predecessors made. Those librarians who have gone through the process are usually very willing to share their expertise with others preparing to enter the world of electronic resources.

It all starts with careful selection and planning. Librarians who carefully weigh the experiences of other libraries offering electronic resources, who consider and prioritize selection criteria, and who have done some homework on the variety of materials available will make the wisest choice and will have a program that makes the transition to electronic resources with relative ease.

One of the first decisions to make is the number of products you will purchase. Most library programs should have an electronic version of an encyclopedia and a magazine index. (It is certainly not written in stone that these products must be purchased, however; a particular library may have excellent reasons for forgoing one or the other.) After that, there are literally thousands of products that can be purchased. As your library begins the selection process, one of the first steps to be taken is to develop a list of the kind of products the library will be first purchasing. Remember that a CD-ROM player can only scan one disk at a time, a modem can only hook into one online database at a time, and a computer can only do one search at a time. It is entirely reasonable to use several products on one computer, but the number that can be shared is limited and must be determined by a judgment of how much use each product will receive.

To begin an electronic information program, it is not necessary to purchase all the computer equipment you will eventually need. Smaller libraries that are just beginning to formulate an electronic information resources program may start with one or two workstations. One station could have a CD encyclopedia and the other a CD magazine index. Those two stations alone would have a tremendous impact on the patrons' use of information. If a modem is placed in each computer, either station could also be used for online searching. As many secondary uses as the library deemed necessary could be placed on the computers. Other CDs or hard-disk-resident databases also could be called up through these computers. However, in a small public or school library, it is important to realize that perhaps as much as 75 percent of the time either the magazine index or the encyclopedia will be in use. The cost-efficiency of any secondary feature most likely will be quite low, simply because it will rarely have a chance to be used.

A large library may inaugurate an electronic resources program with net-worked computers and a menu of choices for the library patron. Even if that is the case, it will still be true that the more general resources will be used most of the time. Very few patrons will exit from the database they are using when they leave the workstation, so a new patron approaching the terminal will have to exit that program and enter, or *launch*, the one that they want to use. The time it takes to exit one program and start up another will be of some concern.

Generally, if a library is planning to put a major electronic source that will be used nearly all of the time on one computer, only one or two secondary uses can be placed on that same computer. If a separate computer workstation is deemed to be for secondary uses only, perhaps four or five uses can be assigned to it.

Regardless of the choices that are made initially, networking the computers will be seen as a viable option before too many years pass. The amount of money needed to network will decrease each year, and it will eventually be seen as an essential expense when the heavy use of the computers makes the stand-alone workstation unwieldy.

ASSESSING YOUR NEEDS

One of the first decisions you will need to make is how many computer terminals you will have. The size of the patron population is a crucial factor. It is helpful to gather as much data as possible on how other libraries have determined the ratio of computer workstations or terminals to patrons. It is always possible to add computers later, so do not feel that the highest figure must be used at the beginning of the program. If a networked environment is planned, it may be simpler to use a range of figures for the number of workstations. Problems can occur if you do not plan for the number of computers that will eventually be used, even if you plan to build up slowly to that figure.

Many of the standards for the number of terminals needed for a given patron population are rather high, especially if patrons are allowed to print the material. When patrons can print the material and take it away from the workstation to peruse, they will spend much less time at the terminal, thus freeing it for other patrons to use. When reading about the number of terminals in a library, realize that two important questions are: "How much of the time are all the terminals in use?" and "How much of the time is there a line waiting to use the terminals?"

The number of library staff is another critical point. At the initial implementation of an electronic resources program, electronic resources are extremely labor-intensive; they will need almost constant attention from library staff. Even after the implementation stage, when staff and the majority of patrons are trained, some products will still require a great deal of attention, especially those that use a great many complicated commands. A product built of various online networks is an example of an extremely labor-intensive operation. Very few libraries will allow patrons to do online searching without a librarian at the patron's elbow. There are other resources, such as some CD-ROMs, that can be left for patron use with minimal library staff attention.

If the library staff is thin, adding electronic resources would be an opportune time to make a case for staff additions. If this is not possible, then the electronic resources purchased should not require much attention. Adding computers to any process does not necessarily save staff time or money. What automation does allow is more and different kinds of research. At times, however, the increased amount of research and accompanying interlibrary loan and other tasks that are generated with an electronic product will actually take more of the librarian's time than before.

PRODUCT EVALUATION

There are a variety of products on the market, and the reasons for purchasing a particular product are as varied as the products themselves. Many times, the reason a particular product was purchased is that it was the first one the librarian saw or it was placed in the library as a trial offer. This is not much of a reason. A resource should be selected on the basis of its value to the library and its patrons. This means researching the market to learn what products are available and what each can do.

When reading, you should make a careful list of the products that are written about. Doing so allows you to make a judgment as to which products will most likely best fit in your library's program. This list will also give some idea of the features available on the products and allow you to compare and contrast the relative merits of a variety of products.

Once a list of possible purchases has been developed, reviews of the print sources can be used to judge the validity of the product's content. Most reviews of the electronic products themselves are not really usable at this stage of the selection process. Too many times, they center on the technology of the product, how many bytes of random access memory (RAM) it uses, and the technology used to develop the resource.

Although the technological aspects of the product are certainly important—after all, one does not want to buy a program incompatible with the existing equipment—they should not be major selection criteria. To put it another way, a book would not be purchased because it was determined that the bindings were extremely well done or even because it had an extensive index. Although these are important factors, they are secondary to whether or not the content of the book is accurate and has value in the library program. It is conceivable that a library would purchase a book with poor bindings or without an index if the value of the product was deemed to be high enough based on content to make up for the factors that were lacking.

With electronic resources, then, the primary consideration must be the impact of the product on the library program. In a school or academic library, this criterion would be the instructional value of the product, its place in the curriculum of the school, or its value to the research interests of the college or university. For a public library, it would be whether or not the product is of reference value in terms of the noted interests of the patron population.

Sometimes it is impossible to determine the content value from a review of the electronic source. There are reviews in which the content of a electronic resource product is only briefly mentioned and the entire focus is on the advanced technology. If the product is based on a print source, then a review of the print source can be used in some ways to determine the electronic version's content, accuracy, and value. After this judgment is made and the product is deemed to have value in the program, then the chart in chapter 3 on the features that should be found in all electronic products can be used. The next factor to be determined is whether full advantage is taken of the possibilities of the electronic format.

If the product is not based on a print source, then great care must be taken to determine the content accuracy of the product. Unlike a book, a CD or online computer cannot be randomly leafed through to test for errors. Instead, the computer equivalent of browsing must be done. This means looking up known facts, easily misspelled words, and other types of common information. During this process, the more easily spotted errors might be found. The data used in the product must have come from somewhere, so checking the authoritativeness of the source facts is also a possibility.

The review of the electronic source can at least be useful in assessing the product's degree of compatibility with the existing computer. Somewhere in the documentation of the computer equipment is a list of features: the type of monitor (i.e., EGA, VGA), the number of bytes of RAM memory, the size of the hard disk, the speed of the modem, and other such information. If you find it difficult to remember this information, carry a card with you or make a copy of that page in the documentation. When you read a review or visit an exhibit, refer to the card to determine the technological needs of the product and see if your hardware is compatible. Do not rule out a purchase if it does not quite meet your needs. Many times the purchase of some small adjustment to the hardware is well worth the cost if it enables the addition of a much-needed resource to the library collection.

**CONSIDERATIONS
FOR READING REVIEWS**

Is the product based on a print source?

What is the authority of the producer?

Is the content accurate?

Is it compatible with existing equipment?

What is the source of the data used in
the product?

Reading

The process of selecting electronic sources starts with reading. Librarians should begin to note in professional journals the stories of other libraries and the products they use. Reading "how I did it in my library" stories is extremely helpful and will provide some idea of both the process and the problems involved. Begin to make some lists of the products you find described in these articles. Compare not only the names of materials purchased but also other factors, such as the size of the patron population and the number of library staff.

READING NOTES	
Name of library	Address
Products used	
Number of terminals	
Number of staff	
Number of patrons	
Other notes	

Talking

Reading stories of other libraries' experiences with electronic resources is the first step in purchasing. After reading several of the articles, you may find that there were questions left unanswered. Perhaps the size of the library or the number of library staff were not mentioned. More often, a problem or positive experience was vaguely referred to but not described in detail. In those cases, the librarian may want to contact the library staff for more details on the product and the problems and positive experiences they have had with it.

Visiting

There may be libraries in your area that have implemented electronic resources. It is not essential at this stage to look for a library similar to yours. A university librarian can benefit from seeing a school or public library that has become automated, and vice versa. The problems and rewards will be the same, simply on a larger or smaller scale. A visit by a select committee helps even more. The committee members could try the materials, observe the ease with which patrons use them, and talk with the staff to learn about the problems of implementation. It is also an excellent opportunity to find out more about the length of time that it took library staff and patrons to become familiar with the use of the materials, the impact of implementing electronic resources on other library programs, and other such information.

Conferences

The last step of the selection process is to use the products themselves. Before taking this step, the librarian in charge of purchases should have a list of materials that have been used successfully in other places and an idea of the number of products that will be used in the library. Deciding the number and mix of products will help prevent poor choices from being made. Conferences are a good place to see a product firsthand. At most conferences there is a bewildering array of products. To the inexperienced librarian just starting the search for electronic information resource, they all will look wonderful. Some will be priced at less than $100, and some will be 20 or 30 times that price. Without a firm grasp of what is needed in a particular library situation, a librarian might purchase a host of minor products on the basis of price alone. The library will not receive the cost-effective benefit of a wise, carefully planned electronic resources program.

Many vendors are quite willing and in fact eager to place their product in a library for a trial period, but this step should not be taken until the very end of the process, when the selection decision has been made or is very close to being made. Electronic resources are wonderful, and a trial resource will be so far superior to the print version that some inexperienced librarians will purchase the first product they see, whether or not it is the best choice. Another reason to wait until near the end of the selection process is that patrons will also be enamored of the first product they have a chance to use and will quickly become skilled in the use of that product. When the product is removed, even if it is replaced by another product with superior capabilities, there may be a howl of protest. A trial period is only useful when the choice has been narrowed to two or three products; then all of the finalists can be brought in for the same trial period, and patrons can evaluate them.

It is better to attend a conference to see the products and make judgments about them. The bigger the conference, the more products that will be on display. Not all vendors exhibit at state conferences, so a national conference is by far the best bet. This is a very cost-efficient way to see all of the new products. Over a four-day exhibit, a prospective purchaser can go back and forth, and actually make several decisions over this time. It would be difficult or impossible to duplicate that experience on a local level.

Before the conference, you should prepare some written charts and question sheets to record the information while you are at the booths. After you leave the exhibits, you will find that things run together in your mind, and it will be impossible to remember just which program offered what feature. Written notes will help you keep everything straight.

Once at the conference, take the questions and charts in hand and set forth. Evaluate each product as if you were a patron too timid to ask the library staff for assistance. As you approach the screen, is it clear to you what you are supposed to do first? This is an especially important question to ask yourself at each stage of the search process.

Remember, most patrons will not find the computer left at the introductory screen with all of the directions. Rather, they will find it wherever the last patron left it— most likely at mid-search. As you are looking at each screen, put yourself in the place of the patron who may walk up to a computer at exactly that point. Does the screen give some indication of how to move from that point—both advancing the search and starting over with a new search? Somewhere on the screen should be simple directions, written in non-computerese, on what keys to hit for the next search. The easier the directions are to follow, the more cost-efficient the resource will be, especially with respect to the factors of patron training and staff time. The training and implementation period will be a disruptive time in the library. A resource that is almost self-explanatory will make that time shorter and smoother.

Wave off the vendor hovering at your elbow and see if, thinking as an inexperienced patron, you can make your way through some simple searches. Refer to the features discussed in chapter 3 and see if they can be performed. You will not find directions to every feature on the screen, but you should be able to have some degree of success, especially with routine search topics.

However, do not let an extremely user-friendly program blind you to its shortcomings. Remember that it will not take long for a user to become expert. Ease of use should be a consideration, but by no means the only one. There should be a level of searching beyond the basic level to provide more access to the database for the experienced user. Ask specific questions on how to do other kinds of searches. Most vendors will then show you the glitzy features the product has. Judge these features harshly in terms of the intended use of the product. If the product is intended for reference and research in a busy library, then the primary purpose is for users to log on to the product, conduct their search, and log off so that another user can have access. Any gadgety procedures such as using bookmarks, drawing x's on a map, or leaving a research trail will greatly slow down that process. Then again, if the intended use is for a learning center in a quiet corner, having pictures and maps may be a wonderful addition, although one user may be sitting at the computer for an hour or more. Keep in mind that the number of users using the product in a given period of time is a measure of cost-efficiency. Keep some sense of how much time each user will be spending on each use.

Features that one librarian may consider glitzy another will find truly useful. It depends in part on the type of library and the type of user. When you are viewing a particular feature, visualize how or if that feature will be used during a typical day in your library.

A conference is also a good place to ask about service, installation help, and search assistance. Hopefully, the vendor will have a toll free help line that is available during normal working hours in all time zones. An 8–5 help line is of little use to a library that has its busiest time during evening and weekend hours.

Most of the time, installation help will be given over the telephone, so keep that in mind when placing the computer in the library. There are times when you will need to be in front of the computer with the telephone in your hand as you follow a step-by-step procedure. Also, ask if a representative will be available to conduct a training session for your staff and whether or not there will be a charge for that training.

Many times at a conference, current users of a product will stop by the booth to discuss their successes, failures, or questions with the vendors. This is a great way to pick up valuable information about a product. Of course, the information will be generally positive, so be sure to ask these users about the size of their library, staff size, and so on. A good strategy is to ask for one good thing and one bad thing about a product.

The goal is to have the list narrowed to two options by the end of the conference. If a product is settled on, the arrangements for a trial period in the library can often be worked out at the conference.

BUYER'S REMORSE

Real estate salespeople know well the concept of buyer's remorse. That is the feeling that sinks in immediately after the settlement that says that we have made a terrible mistake, that it was not really the best purchase, that something else will come on the market tomorrow that exactly fits our needs, and why, oh why, did we buy this?

In a library program, you are spending someone else's money, which makes that feeling ten times worse. True, something may well come on the market tomorrow that is ten times better than what you just purchased. The consolation here is that when products are purchased that are industry standards, both in hardware and software, upgrading to the latest change on the market is both relatively painless and relatively inexpensive.

Instead of focusing on what you could or should have purchased, think instead of the change that has been made from the information service that you offered before the addition of electronic products to the service that you offer now. Your program is never finished, just as the library collection is never complete. A growing, changing electronic resources program will consist of the best choices available at the time of purchase, with an eye for new additions to the program.

5

Selection of a
CD Encyclopedia

As discussed in an earlier chapter, most library programs would benefit from having an electronic version of an encyclopedia. Just as a print encyclopedia is a general reference tool for library patrons, an encyclopedia in electronic form can be the central part of an electronic resources program. Because it does add such a great deal to a library program, there are specific criteria that apply just to this type of electronic resource.

Although electronic encyclopedias are available in many formats, most libraries will find an encyclopedia on CD-ROM their most cost-effective choice. Therefore, this chapter focuses on CD-ROM encyclopedias, although the process can be applied to the purchase of any type of electronic encyclopedia.

An electronic version of an encyclopedia becomes more of a multipurpose reference tool than a print encyclopedia can be. Because virtually every word in the electronic encyclopedia can be searched for, users can perform searches that are impossible in the print version. It is possible, for example, to search for the word "first" beside the word "woman" to find a list of subjects for women's studies, or to find every occurrence of a word or phrase for bibliometric or linguistic uses.

Librarians are constantly referring patrons to encyclopedias as a starting point for research. The electronic version will provide an excellent overview for this purpose, because the approach is basically that of an index. In fact, one can think of an electronic version of an encyclopedia as the print version with the best index possible, one that lists virtually every word included in the resource.

CD OR ONLINE?

There are computerized encyclopedias available in both CD and online versions; one is now even available on videodisc. The videodisc encyclopedia is relatively new, and the technology promises to be exciting. However, it is still rather expensive. At present, an index to images on the videodisc encyclopedia can be searched, and the text can be searched. When images themselves can be input for searching against a database of images, the videodisc encyclopedia will find its true value as a reference tool. If a library has an extensive multimedia program, the videodisc encyclopedia would have some value now.

Most libraries of any size are better off buying the CD-ROM encyclopedia and using the online encyclopedia as a secondary source. The CD encyclopedia is a universal reference tool and has a variety of uses. Many patrons will find a number of uses for it, and some will find it enjoyable to browse through for subject words to look up. This is especially true of school-age patrons. With a CD version, this kind of "play" is a good way to get patrons familiar with electronic searching. Online searching costs money each time the patron logs on, severely limiting this kind of practice searching. Because such practice is so valuable to younger patrons, purchasing only an online encyclopedia is not a cost-effective choice for most school and public libraries.

The CD version of the encyclopedia can be left relatively unattended, and patrons can search at will with little supervision. This browsing greatly increases the search skills of patrons, allows patrons to become more comfortable with the technology, and is an excellent serendipitous learning tool. Very few patrons will be seen leafing through the pages of a print encyclopedia to see what subjects are covered, yet they often do the equivalent with a CD encyclopedia.

BEGINNING THE SEARCH

There are various ways to begin a search for a CD encyclopedia. One good way to start is similar to how one would start when buying a print encyclopedia: with the reviews. Because most encyclopedias are based on a print source, reading published reviews of the print version is helpful. An encyclopedia that received poor reviews as a print source probably will not improve in the switch to an electronic source.

Evaluating
Electronic Encyclopedias

The major points of a print encyclopedia review—such as the accuracy, depth and breadth of coverage in the various subjects, authority of the authors of the articles, and currency of the information—are also of vital importance in reviews of the electronic version. In addition to these factors, pay close attention to the amount of changes made with each upgrade. A CD encyclopedia can be either bought outright or leased, a concept that was further discussed in an earlier chapter. If the library must purchase an upgrade each year in order to keep the product, it would be helpful to know how much of a change there is from year to year. One good point about the yearly upgrades is that they are relatively inexpensive, especially when compared to the cost of an updated print encyclopedia. Most libraries will find that to the extent the CD encyclopedia is used, the print encyclopedias will not have to be replaced as quickly. In fact, the purchase of a CD encyclopedia may even pay for itself through reductions in the expenditures for print encyclopedias.

However, the purchase of a CD-ROM encyclopedia is a long-term investment, and the yearly upgrades are almost a form of blackmail. That is, even though a librarian may become dissatisfied with the encyclopedia, the fact that it can be updated for less than $200 will make it difficult to justify switching to another CD and paying the initial fee, which may be three or four times the price of the upgrade. Therefore, the choice of initial purchase must be made carefully; librarians will be reluctant to "change brands" and start over again with another large investment.

Carefully check the reading level of the encyclopedia. Even though the resource is computerized, the text will still have to be read by the patron, either from the screen or from the printout. Reading difficulties for CD encyclopedias range from collegiate to elementary school level. Make sure that you buy a product that can be read and understood by the majority of the patrons in your library.

It is worth checking the quality of the indexing of the print source. Although the searching capabilities of the computer make the print index a moot point, a poorly compiled index in the print version will not breed confidence in the quality of the electronic version.

The CD encyclopedia cannot be leafed through page by page, so it is essential that users are able to find exactly what they want, rather than something close enough. The margin of error that makes the difference between finding information and being told by the computer that no information exists on the subject is very narrow.

Typographical errors should be limited or nonexistent, and there should be consistency in the use of words

---

QUESTIONS FOR ELECTRONIC ENCYCLOPEDIA EVALUATION

Is there a print review?

What is the reading level?

How often is it upgraded?

What is the price for the upgrade?

Must you purchase each upgrade as it is offered?

Boolean searching?

Onscreen dictionary?

Truncation?

---

with variant spellings (such as marijuana, AIDS, and so on). Certainly, in casual browsing at an exhibit, you should find few, if any, errors. If you spot several in a five-minute session, extrapolate that to imagine how many errors could possibly be in the entire product.

Learning from Other
Libraries

The second step in buying an electronic product is usually reading articles about the implementation process and talking to librarians that own the product. This latter step, although important when buying most types of electronic resources, does not always bring accurate information when buying a CD encyclopedia, for several reasons.

When CD encyclopedias first came on the market, there was only one product available for quite a few years. Because upgrades may be purchased for a low price, many libraries have stayed with the original product, regardless of whether or not a newer encyclopedia might suit their present needs better. Another product is now available for a low price when bought in combination with the print version of the product. Again, libraries may be buying this CD because of that arrangement.

There is certainly nothing wrong with either of these products, and libraries are certainly justified in purchasing them for the reasons given. The only caution to be raised is that the purchases were not made because of the product's instructional value to the library program. Anytime a library makes a reference purchase for any reason other than that it is the best product for the program, great care needs to be taken in using that library's experience as a selection criterion. Ideally, the product should best fit the needs of the user rather than the convenience of the library budget.

It may be wise to ask some additional questions. Some of these questions might be: Monetary questions aside, what other products did you look at, and which ones would you buy if money were not an issue? Another important question is: If you were buying one today, would you stick with this product or shop around for one that better fits your needs?

Hands-on Testing
at Conferences

Conference visits are extremely worthwhile when shopping for a CD encyclopedia. Because there are relatively few CD encyclopedia products, it should be fairly simple to narrow the choices down at a conference where all of them are exhibiting. It is well worth a trip to a national conference to do this, because not all of the vendors offering CD encyclopedias will be attending state or regional conferences.

Most major CD vendors are also willing to place a product in a library for a trial period. Be careful with this offer. Any electronic encyclopedia will seem wonderful in comparison with a print source. Take this step near the end of your search, when you are fairly sure that you have made your selection. A trial period is a double-check, rather than a preliminary step.

ENCYCLOPEDIAS
AND SEARCH MODES

In any electronic resource tool, there are two main ways of searching: the browse mode and the word search mode. (These modes are described more fully in chapter 3.)

In browse mode, the user types in a search term and the computer responds with an alphabetic list of the subjects or titles that most closely match that word (see fig. 5.1). One advantage of this method is that if the user misspells the search word, it is still possible that the displayed list will contain the correct heading, as long as the user has typed the first letters correctly. A disadvantage is that only article titles are searched. The user must be aware that if the word entered does not appear in any article titles, it does not necessarily mean that the computer has no information on that subject. In most cases, it simply means that the information on that topic is contained within an article (or articles) that uses other words in the title. Many inexperienced users will not be aware of this and will simply assume that the encyclopedia has no information on that topic. Even worse, the patron will have a negative reaction to the product and possibly to electronic products in general. To avoid this undesirable outcome, the library staff can do several things to educate patrons about alternative methods of searching. Posting signage on a bulletin board behind the product, preparing handouts for patrons to follow when using the product, or simply being extra observant to see if someone is having trouble are some strategies that can be used very successfully.

```
ALT File    Edit    Tools    Windows    Options    Help          O OO



IM5Browse TitlesFMMMMMMMMMMMMMMMMMMMMMMMMMMMMMMMMMMMMMM4/3420MMQM;
: 6th Amendment                                              31:
: 7th Amendment              IMMMMMMMMMMMMMMMMMMMMMMM;  :
: 8th Amendment              : [                    ] :  :
: 9th Amendment              HMMMMMMMMMMMMMMMMMMMMMM<  :
: A                                                  3 :
: Aachen                                             3 :
: Aakjaer, Jeppe                                     3 :
: Aalborg:                                           3 :
: Aalto, Alvar                                       3:
HMMMMMMMMMMMMMMMMMMMMMMMMMMMMMMMMMMMMMMMMMMMMMMMMMMMMMMMMMMMMMMMOM<


            To find entry, type the first letter(s)
              of an article title and press ENTER.
```

Fig. 5.1. Browse Mode for Titles. From the *Academic American Encyclopedia*, electronic version. Copyright 1993 by Grolier Incorporated. Reprinted by permission.

In many ways, the browse method could be performed using a print encyclopedia, because it merely goes to the list of article titles. The word search mode, by contrast, cannot be duplicated in a print source, because the computer looks at the actual text of the article.

In the word search mode, the computer searches the CD-ROM to find a word or combination of words specified by the user. The biggest problem that patrons have with this mode of searching is that they tend to input far too many words and thus return with no "hits." For instance, suppose a patron wants information on women astronauts who flew in outer space. A search for "women" and "astronaut" may be sufficient. Inexperienced patrons, however, may search for "women" and "astronaut" and "outer space" and "flying" and maybe even some other words thrown in for good measure. This search could be successful, but the great number of search words will most likely eliminate some useful articles.

Another danger of the word search mode is that patrons also tend to confuse the Boolean operators *and* and *or* which will also lead to no hits. Truncation can also be misused in a full-text source. Patrons tend to truncate the word too early. Searching for "cat*," for instance, will produce results ranging in variety from "catastrophic" to "catatonic."

Embedded truncation—using truncation in the middle of a word to substitute for any letter—is a helpful feature in word search mode. Some products also offer truncation at the beginning of a word. This is a rather unique option that has limited use, but in a school setting it is conceivable that it could be helpful—to provide teachers with list of words that end in "tion," for example. Another possible use would be to help users who are unsure of the spelling of the first part of their search word.

A popular feature in the word search mode is the use of *proximity operators*. These enable the user to direct the computer to search for words that are directly beside each other, in the same sentence, or in the same paragraph. In most CD encyclopedias these operators are not symbols but rather choices from a pull-down menu (see fig. 5.2).

```
ALT File    Edit    Tools    Windows    Options    Help                 0 02
                        IM5Search OptionsFMMMMMMMM;
                        :      BEGIN SEARCH        :
IM5WORD  SEARCHFMMMMMMMMMMMMMMMMGDDDDDDDDDDDDDDDDDDDDDDDDDDDD6MMMMMMMMMMMMMMMMM;
:  Type search word or words th:  Search In:           :press ENTER.        :
GDDDDDDDDDDDDDDDDDDDDDDDDDDDDDDD:  Article Titles       :DDDDDDDDDDDDDDDDDD6
:  Word(s) [                    :  Article Text         :          )         :
:    with [                     :  Picture Captions     :          )         :
:    with [                     :  Bibliographies       :          )         :
:    with [                     :  Factboxes            :          )         :
:                               :                       :                    :
HMMMMMMMMMMMMMMMMMMMMMMMMMMMMMMM:  Word Relationship:    :MMMMMMMMMMMMMMMMMMM(
:                               :  In Same Article      :
:                               :  In Same Paragraph    :
:                               :  Words Apart [10]     :
:                               :  Exact Order          :
:                               :                       :
:                               :  Negate Search Line   :
                        HMMMMMMMMMMMMMMMMMMMMMMMMMMMMM(
```

```
        Highlight the option you wish to change then press ENTER.
               Press ESC to return to search.
```

Fig. 5.2. Pull-down Menu. From the *Academic American Encyclopedia*, electronic version. Copyright 1993 by Grolier Incorporated. Reprinted by permission.

Uses of Search Modes

In a school setting, CD-ROM searches can be used both to teach the use of the product and as an innovative reading assignment. For example, a class can be assigned to find three things that happened on their birthday. A search for their birth month beside their birthday ("June" beside "10," say) will find all occurrences of that date in the encyclopedia. Even high school students cannot resist reading most of the articles to find the "coolest" list of three things.

In a public or academic setting, a list of sample searches should include some that are "fun" for beginning users to perform. These will encourage people to try a search, and it is by doing some of these things that patrons will become familiar with the product. Very soon after a product has been installed in a library, patrons will become expert at its use—in fact, more expert than the library staff. Products that offer sophisticated search modes that add to the research value of the product and increase the speed and efficiency of the search are worthwhile purchases.

Important in the discussion of search modes is the default mode that the vendor has chosen for the primary method of searching. As discussed earlier, the primary mode is the one that users would achieve if they simply hit the enter key at each screen requiring a choice. Many users will do just that rather than arrowing up or down to another choice, especially when they are first learning how to use the product. Many encyclopedias use the word search mode as the primary search mode. If a library purchases one of these CD encyclopedias, then training patrons in the use of the word search mode should become a high priority. Many patrons will find the intricacies of Boolean searching and truncation very difficult at first. Care must be taken that some patrons are not turned off to the idea of electronic searching because of a confusing experience on their first try.

CHECKLIST
FOR EVALUATION

The following can be used as a checklist for the evaluation of the features in a CD encyclopedia.

Screen

The opening screen should be eye-catching but not cluttered. Directions for the required user input should be clearly noted on the screen. Most software programs use the enter key to move the program forward and the escape key (Esc) to go backwards. It is helpful if those same keys make logical sense in a CD-ROM encyclopedia.

For some reason, some CD encyclopedias place the text in a box in the middle of the screen, with empty space around the box. Apart from the reason that having fewer words on the screen makes it look less intimidating, there is really no reason to do this. A better choice is a product that has text on one half of the screen and the index to the article on the other side. As the user scrolls down on one side, the other side moves accordingly.

Note the size of the typeface and the space between lines. Some people have difficulty reading from a computer screen. A screen with bigger type may seem easier to read. Also, some programs have a setup mode in which the screen colors can be changed. Although some people will find certain colors easier to read than others, computer-adept users will find it an interesting pastime to change the colors and may do so frequently.

The menu should allow the patron to move from one search mode to another with minimal confusion. Some encyclopedias have other search options besides browse and word search. The usefulness of these choices in a busy reference area must be judged according to the typical kinds of information requests that patrons have. Generally, the two search modes and a word index (if there is one) are enough; having further choices may be confusing to the user. Options such as having the user plot a point on a map, then zoom into the location and pull up information about that city, state, or country, are very close to being educational games rather than a research activity. This is not necessarily negative, but it does lead one to wonder why the patron does not just type in the name of the desired geographic location in the first place.

Moreover, having more than two choices means that the user will spend much more time on the machine, because several blind alleys will most likely be followed at first. In a busy library, it will be impossible not to notice that the first 10 minutes of the search were wasted while other patrons waited to use the product. However, in a quieter area of the library, this kind of browsing may be of great value. The purpose of the product within the library setting has to be a primary criterion in selecting the best encyclopedia for any library program.

Indexing

Most electronic databases have a list of words that are not indexed. These are commonly called *stopwords*. Usually these are words such as *a*, *it*, *by*, and so forth. These non-indexed words are more noticeable in a full-text source such as an encyclopedia, which uses more of the common one- and two-letter words. This is rather important when searching an encyclopedia or any full-text product, because words that appear over and over in the encyclopedia will greatly slow down the search. The documentation should contain a list of words that are not indexed in the product. The list should be long enough to include most of the words (such as those above) that would not be used in the search process. Sometimes, however, product developers go overboard in the stopword area. There was a product that, in its early version, decided not to index single-digit numbers or letters. It probably seemed like a good idea at the time, until the product was sold and users realized that this indexing decision meant they could search for "World War II" but not "World War I." Users could find information on Richard II, III, IV, or VI but not on Richard I or Richard V.

When a user inputs a stopword as part of the search, the computer simply ignores it. In the search above for "Richard I" or "Richard V," the computer would simply find all Richards listed in the source—including anyone mentioned whose first name happened to be Richard. The computer cannot translate numbers into letters unless programmed to do so. Thus, if the search phrase is "World War II," references to "World War *Two*" would not be retrieved. It is hoped that the encyclopedia being searched is consistent enough not to use "World War Two" in the text.

A word index is simply a list of all words indexed in the product. This is essential when searching scientific or medical terms, which sometimes have several viable spellings and word endings. It is also a good way to double-check the search term when a search reports that the word entered is not in the encyclopedia. Very few words are not in the encyclopedia, and any search that produces zero hits should be suspect. The word index should then be used to check spelling and look for variant forms of the word.

Displaying and Printing

Users should be able to choose between printing the article or saving it to disk for later printing. Other options include the ability to print a single page or paragraph of the article (see fig. 5.3, p. 54). Certainly the length of the article should be noted on the screen before printing. There is a great deal of time difference between printing a one-paragraph article and one that may be 20 pages in length.

```
ALT File    Edit    Tools    Windows    Options    Help                    O 05
IMFileFMMMMMMMMMMMMMMMM;
: Print                            :
: Save                             :
: Load NotePad          :nn BennettFMMMMMMMMMMMMMMMMMMMMMMMMMMMMMMMMMM1/2MMOM;
: Save NotePad          :n Bennett                                         3 :
: Quit                  :                                                  3 :
HMMMMMMMMMMMMMMMMMMMMMMM(d. b. Royalton, N.Y., Oct. 24, 1830, d. May 19, 3 :
                        : 1917, was the first woman lawyer admitted to practice before the 31:
                        : U.S. Supreme Court and the first woman candidate for the U.S.   3 :
                        : presidency. Rejected by many law schools on the ground that she  3 :
                        : was a woman, she finally entered the National University Law     3 :
                        : School and was admitted to the District of Columbia bar in 1873. 3 :
                        : She won the right to present cases before the Supreme Court in   3 :
                        : 1879. Lockwood was a leading litigator and lobbyist on behalf of 3 :
                        : women's rights. In 1884 and 1888 she was nominated as the        3 :
                        : presidential candidate of the National Equal Rights party.       3:
HMMMMMMMMMMMMMMMMMMMMMMMMMMMMMMMMMMMMMMMMMMMMMMMMMMMMMMMMMMMMMMMMMMMMMMMMMOM(

Use CURSOR keys to move through article. +/- key for next/previous article.
Press TAB to move to next Search Word occurrence. Press Alt-L for Link
```

Fig. 5.3. Print and Save Options. From the *Academic American Encyclopedia*, electronic version. Copyright 1993 by Grolier Incorporated. Reprinted by permission.

Another feature usually offered is the ability to mark sections of text and then move the section directly to a word processor, a procedure called *exporting*. This is a highly touted feature for some products, but it is questionable whether patrons actually use it on a regular basis. Before buying a product that offers such features, try to evaluate what users would want that feature and whether or not it is really an important criterion for purchase. The simple fact that the technology allows a process to occur is not necessarily a sufficient reason to purchase it if there is little patron need for the process.

A feature in some of the newer encyclopedias is a dictionary. The user can highlight a word and press the enter key, and the definition of the word will appear. Test this by looking up several common words to see if you can find one that does not have an included definition.

Speed

Comparing the speed of various products is another consideration. Be careful to note the time it takes you as a user to complete a search from beginning to end. Start from the time you walk up to the computer and end when you are printing your search results. A common error is to time only the speed at which the computer searches a topic. A librarian needs to take a broader perspective and consider the average time one user will spend at the computer.

You might also want to note how long it takes the CD-ROM to boot up, especially if you have one CD-ROM player and you plan to use a variety of products. Time the computer from when you turn it on until the time the product is ready for the first input.

A WORD ABOUT PICTURES

Some encyclopedias that are now coming out have pictures. The usefulness of this feature should be judged against the inefficiency of having an individual user spend too much time at the computer browsing through pictures that could be found elsewhere while preventing another user with a valid research need from using the CD.

The availability of pictures (and sometimes accompanying sounds) has increased the difficulty of making a wise selection for a CD-ROM encyclopedia. Many librarians are using this as a primary selection criterion and not considering encyclopedias that do not include pictures. When such a factor is seen as this important, then the purpose of purchasing a CD encyclopedia must be reviewed. Several questions arise:

Can You Print the Pictures? In most cases, the equipment used in the library means that the answer is no. Even if that is a future consideration, printing any sort of graphic takes an incredible amount of time. Five or ten minutes is not uncommon, and some graphics take much longer. And even with a color printer and unlimited time, the pictures used in the encyclopedia are full color and would not print well.

How Will Patrons Use the Pictures? In most cases, they will simply look at them. Most of the pictures in the electronic encyclopedia are not similar to those found in print encyclopedias, which are simply used to enhance points made in the text. The CD pictures are beautiful full-screen illustrations that stand on their own. For instance, the article on dogs is accompanied by screen after screen of pictures of individual dog breeds. Such a feature is very popular with students, who will sit at the computer for an hour or more and look at pictures of dogs. This is an excellent use of the CD as a learning station in a quiet corner of the library. But in a busy reference center, with patrons queuing up to use the workstations, it will greatly increase the amount of time one patron spends at one machine.

What Is the Research Value of the Pictures? Very rarely will the pictures be used for research of any kind, even casual research. In a print encyclopedia, pictures are used as examples or illustrations of points made in the text. One article may have several pictures of various sizes, some in color and some not. Most of the graphics in print encyclopedias are line drawings or photographs, and almost all of the articles have some type of accompanying graphic.

In CD encyclopedias, the pictures are generally not there to illustrate points made in the text; most of the articles do not even have pictures. Although a salesman can come up with a multitude of perfectly rational situations in which patrons will absolutely need those pictures that are contained in the CD resource, most of the time the patron would be better served by printing the article on the workstation, then finding an appropriate book on the library shelves for the pictures.

The same is true for sound. If a cassette tape of birdcalls is available for $8.95, it is difficult to imagine spending $3,000 so that one patron can sit with headphones and listen to the same thing. Unless the library can afford a multitude of computer learning stations that give patrons an opportunity to browse through and play with the added features, buying a product that has them will greatly decrease the cost-effectiveness of the product.

The one advantage of pictures and sound is the addition of multimedia instruction. The pictures and sound can be combined with videodisc images to develop multimedia presentations. Even here, however, it might be wise to consider the use of the product in a library setting. A multimedia learning station is an excellent use of resources, but it is doubtful that such a station will be the central focus of the reference area.

CONCLUSION

As more and more encyclopedias are presented in electronic form, library media specialists will have to be consistent in setting guidelines for selection of these sources to find the product best suited to an individual library program. Any feature that would detract from the serious research use of the product—which means entering a search, finding an article, and printing—is moving from research use into an educational game. An educational game is not harmful in itself, but each product should be carefully assessed as to the future use in a specific library program.

6

Selection of Magazine Indexes

Almost any type of library has a magazine index of some variety, whether in the traditional print format or an electronic format. Almost all research that is done in a library—be it a school, public, or academic library—involves some use of a magazine index.

Using a print magazine index is time consuming and tedious, and the process begs for automation. Patrons must look through several annual volumes and monthly updates in order to conduct a thorough search for articles; then they must paper-and-pencil copy the tiny print in order to find the information with which to request the article.

The importance of an electronic magazine index in a library program has been established through several years of experience. Now, as one walks through the exhibit area at a major conference, it is easy to see that there is competition in the field, and there are many options from which to choose the electronic magazine index best suited to an individual library program.

An electronic magazine index that directs patrons to articles on various topics has a definite impact on a library program. Such an index can triple the use of magazines and greatly increase the amount of interlibrary loan requests. The factors to consider in deciding to buy an electronic magazine index are varied and include not only deciding which vendor to use but also whether to buy a product with full text, bibliographic citations only, bibliographic citations with accompanying microfiche, or bibliographic citations with abstracts.

ONLINE
VERSUS CD-ROM

The choice between subscribing to an online magazine index versus purchasing a CD-ROM index must be considered in terms of the use of the product. Although a CD-ROM magazine index may be more expensive, it may be the better choice in the long run. Most libraries will not allow patrons, at least initially, to search online without professional assistance. Therefore, the cost of an online index is compounded by the time and effort the library staff must spend helping patrons to perform searches. The CD-ROM index usually needs minimal supervision and can be left at a browsing station for patron use. For that reason, the CD-ROM magazine index is probably the better purchase in most cases.

Generally speaking, only the very smallest libraries will want to forgo the purchase of a CD magazine index in favor of an online service. However, an online magazine index is an excellent secondary resource to have in addition to the CD-ROM, especially if it is a different product, because it provides an alternative with which to find information on very specific and obscure subjects.

BEGINNING THE SEARCH

The standard print magazine index can be described as a bibliographic list of magazine articles indexed by subject. With the electronic versions, there are many alternatives for the patron. Each provides a different type and amount of information. There are valid arguments for and against indexes that are full text, bibliographic, bibliographic plus microfiche, and bibliographic plus abstracts. The impact of each type of magazine index will vary.

A bibliographic magazine index is a list of citations similar to the information found in a print magazine index. With the bibliographic list, patrons will find 15 to 20 citations and will actually request perhaps half that many articles. Searching in a bibliographic magazine index is usually faster than searching in a full-text product. At extremely busy times, the library staff can supervise the process of searching a bibliographic index to make it work most efficiently. One patron will input a subject, hit enter, and then begin printing the citations while the next patron is inputting another search topic. The first patron can take his or her printout away from the workstation and review it at leisure before requesting the articles from the library shelves. Of all the types of magazine indexes, a bibliographic source generally will involve the least amount of time spent at the machine and the least amount of paper, and patrons will end up using the most articles.

In a full-text source, the patron searches for and retrieves a number of articles and usually reviews them onscreen before choosing perhaps three or four for printing. Most workstations will be configured to allow another patron to begin the search once the printing has started, but it will take some time to print several articles, depending on their length. . With a full-text source, patrons are able to tell exactly if a given article meets their needs, but they will take longer on the machine and will use a great deal more paper than with the bibliographic index. The number of articles used will probably not increase much from the amount that patrons used with the print source.

There are other choices as well. Some bibliographic indexes now have abstracts. Here again, patrons will be able to make better choices and tell if the articles will exactly meet their needs but will take longer at the computer while reviewing the abstracts. Even after the patron chooses which citations to print, the articles still have to be requested from the library shelves.

Finally, some sources come with accompanying microfiche. The question librarians should consider before investing in such a source is how much duplication there is between the microfiche and their own collection. A library with a fair collection of the most heavily used journals may find that a simple bibliographic tool meets their needs. A library that is just being built and has no back issues of periodicals may think it wise to invest in a full-text source or a bibliographic source with microfiche.

Some indexes have accompanying newspaper articles on microfiche. For libraries that generally do not keep back issues of newspapers, one of these may be a wise choice.

Literature Review

After consideration is given the various types of magazine indexes, the next step is a quick review of the literature. There have been various descriptive articles of how magazine indexes are used in all types of libraries. These reports can give the librarian some idea of the product's typical use and its impact in a library program.

With the proliferation of electronic resources in libraries, it should not be difficult to find a library similar to yours that has some sort of an electronic magazine index. It may be helpful to call that library and request a visit or simply discuss the implementation of the source over the phone. Sometimes that will save you a great deal of time and money, to say nothing of frustration.

Most magazine indexes are based on print sources, so a check through the literature for the review of the print source is always helpful. There are published reviews of most electronic sources, but these reviews are almost always positive, if not glowing. A better perspective is usually obtained in the review of the research value of the corresponding *print* product. Certainly comments on the indexing, accuracy, and completeness of the source will apply to the electronic source.

Reviews of the electronic source can be helpful in the areas of ease of use and hardware compatibility. The electronic reviews can also be used to double-check vendor claims.

USING ELECTRONIC
MAGAZINE INDEXES

Armed with data and a preliminary understanding of the use and impact of the source, the next step is to look at the actual product. The best place to do so is at a state or national conference. Although vendors are quite willing to install their product in a library for a trial period, you should agree to this only after you have decided on a particular product.

Using a print magazine index is time consuming and requires the use of several different books and copying of citations. When an electronic magazine index is placed in a library for the first time, it will be judged only in comparison with the cumbersome print source. The electronic source will quickly become an essential part of the library program, with all patrons becoming skilled at its use. Removing it, even to replace it with another magazine index, will be difficult, if not impossible, even if another source would be a better choice for the program. Therefore, it is crucial to select a source that will fit your library's needs over the long term.

At a large conference, several types of electronic magazine indexes are displayed. It is possible to go from one to the other several times, comparing and evaluating the use and the ease of various features. Some of these products may not be considered magazine indexes in the traditional sense. However, you should probably look at any product that indexes magazine or journal articles as part of its operating capability. Keep an open mind about a product you may not have initially considered. Sometimes it may turn out to be your best choice.

Not all of the librarians visiting the vendors are shopping. Some of them already own the product and are stopping by to ask questions or to comment on the product's implementation. Most of these experienced users are quite willing to share information, such as how they use the source, the impact it has had on the total library program, and what other sources they have in the library.

As you walk up to the computer at a conference, the vendor will be quick to assist in the use of the product and may in fact demonstrate it for you. Don't be shy about asking the vendor to go back to a previous screen if it has flashed by too quickly for you to read it completely. If you would like to use the product yourself and try to figure out what to do next by screen directions alone, ask the vendor to allow you to use it uninterrupted.

When testing a product, put yourself in the place of a patron who is seeing the source for the first time. How easily can you determine what to do next? Does the product grab your attention and invite you to try it? A user-friendly computer screen has few words and lots of open space. The screen should be eye-catching yet uncluttered, with the first input that is required clearly noted on the screen. The typeface should be fairly large and easy to read. Certainly the essential directions of what to do next, or what choices the user has, should be on each screen.

A magazine index is one of the most heavily used references in the library. It is essential that the source chosen has complete onscreen directions. Most libraries do not have staff to stand by the machines and help each patron.

Searching

As noted earlier, there are two main search avenues to any electronic database—browse mode and word search mode. In electronic magazine indexes, browse mode is essentially an index to subject headings, with any subheadings displayed along with the main topic. The number of citations found under each heading also is usually displayed.

This feature has an added bonus for school and academic libraries in that it helps patrons narrow research topics. The student can see immediately which subtopics have enough information to be valid areas for research. For faculty members, this will also provide an excellent outline of a topic, displaying the important points that should be covered in an overview.

From this screen, a CD-ROM product should list *see* and *see also* references. If the word the patron enters is not used as a subject heading by that database, the product should note that the subject can be found through another topic. Avoid products that do not have this capability. For instance, if the patron enters the subject heading of "drunk drivers" and the correct term is actually under the heading of "alcohol use," this should be noted. If no explanations or alternatives are given, the patron may walk away in frustration. Ask the vendor how a patron will know the proper subject heading if they enter the wrong one.

Even if the patron finds some hits with the chosen subject word, there should be a way for the product to show related topics. The *see* and *see also* reference lists should be accessible at the touch of a key.

For word search mode, the product documentation should note which fields are searched. If the source has abstracts or full text, it would be helpful if those fields could be searched also. The more fields searched, the more complete the search and the greater the chance of finding citations.

Some sources allow the patron to select which fields can be searched. The choices of author, subject, and title are listed on the screen. Experiment to see what will happen if the patron puts the same word on each line. For instance, if a patron is researching Edgar Allan Poe, he or she will want articles that are by and about Poe, as well as those that include the word "Poe" in the title. There is an implied "or" between the title, author, and subject lines. It is helpful if the product allows users to specify this in their searches; it will save time if the can do a single search to find articles either by *or* about their subject. The database product will designate one of these search modes (i.e., browse or word search) as the primary mode, with the other being secondary. In an electronic magazine index, the browse search mode is preferable as a primary search mode for several reasons. It is much easier for patrons to use, and it allows for very satisfactory searching for most general research questions. Most patrons will be able to figure out the browse mode almost immediately. The word search mode, by contrast, requires some knowledge of the theory of database searching.

Although it is true that the database will probably offer both types of searching, patrons will be using the product independently for much of the time in a busy library. If the browse mode is the primary method of searching, the patron will have a much higher success rate and will require much less attention from the library staff.

Display and Printing

After a search has been conducted and the screen is showing the list of subjects found, the user should be able to select a subject and bring the full citations to the screen by simply hitting the enter key. Long combinations of keystrokes are a waste of time. In a busy library, patrons must be able to type in the subject, hit enter, arrow up or down to a chosen heading, hit enter again, see if the first citation is on target, start a list of citations printing, then move off for another patron. Extra steps slow down the process and create frustration for the experienced user. By the same token, if the printer has a problem (e.g., it runs out of paper or is offline), the product should display an error message instead of freezing up or ignoring the problem. The user should then be able to correct the problem or cancel the print process and start over.

When you are reviewing the citations list on the screen, examine it carefully. It should be easy to read, with enough open space that users of all reading levels do not feel intimidated. The author, title of the article, magazine title and issue, and number of pages should be clearly noted and easy to distinguish. Evaluate this from the viewpoint of the user, but also evaluate it for completeness from a librarian's point of view. Make sure that the information a librarian will need to retrieve a magazine or request an article on interlibrary loan is listed.

If the source does not have abstracts or full text, the citation is most helpful if it displays the subject headings on the screen. Patrons will find that if they review the subject headings of citations that best fit their search topic, they can do another, more complete search using those headings. The displayed subject headings also give a far more detailed indication of the content of the article than does the title alone. In this way, the subject headings can be viewed as a kind of mini-abstract of the article.

Two print options are fairly standard for a magazine index. The first is to print one citation at a time. With this method, the user can review each citation as it appears, printing some and bypassing others. When no one else is waiting to use the computer, this is an acceptable method. The other print option is to print the entire list of citations. This is especially helpful when all of the citations seem to be pertinent to the search topic or when there are patrons waiting to use the computer. Even though there may be a few hundred citations, this print mode can be useful. After twenty or so citations are printed, the escape key (Esc) can be used to stop the printing.

Some products now have a limit on the number of citations that print at any one time, although the limit can usually be changed in the program setup. This means that even when the patron chooses the "print all" mode, perhaps 20 citations will print, and then the computer will ask if the user wants 20 more printed. Regardless of the print mode chosen, the user should be able to start the printing process with one keystroke. It is assumed that there will be a printer attached to every workstation. To have patrons finding citations in seconds is rather useless if they still have to copy down the citation from the screen by hand while other patrons are queuing up behind them.

QUESTIONS TO ASK

The following questions may be helpful in selecting the CD-ROM magazine index. There are no right answers, and a vendor will probably not be able to give the answer you want to hear for every question. A librarian making the choice of an electronic magazine index will have to weigh the pros and cons of each response and give more weight to the criteria that are most important to that library program.

Is There a Print Version? Most electronic magazine indexes are based on a print version of the same name. This may be a preference for your library program, because patrons will already be familiar with subject headings, indexing style, and other factors.

What Are the Dates of Inclusion? You should not have to ask this question. The years covered by the source should be clearly noted on the computer screen. If the product is a CD-ROM, a follow-up question to this one is: How much room is left on the CD? Each year, as another CD is produced with another year's worth of titles, will the years of coverage be increased, or will a year of coverage be deleted?

Consider the impact of the answer to this question on your periodical collection. If the index covers everything back to 1983, as one popular source does, then you must assume that patrons could be requesting magazines back to 1983. Does your library have periodicals that old? The value of access to very old citations is decided by whether or not your collection includes the years indexed.

How Often Is the CD-ROM Disk Updated? There are many subquestions in this category. Certainly you may want to ask how many citations are added in an average update. You will also want to know how long it takes before current information is indexed and placed on the CD. You can check on this by searching a topic currently in the news and finding the date of the most recent citation.

When a CD-ROM is updated, the software sometimes changes; publishers do tend to keep fiddling with their products. The changes are usually minor, but it means that the software installed on the computer has to be updated. You might want to know how many times past updates have required the software to be reinstalled.

Do I Buy or Lease the Product? When you buy a CD-ROM product, it is yours to keep, regardless of what choices you make in succeeding years. You should be allowed to keep outdated disks, even if you choose not to buy subsequent updates. If you have a legitimate purpose for the outdated disks, the vendor should be made aware of this use and approve of it. In some instances, it may be illegal to keep outdated disks. The ethics of our profession require that we look askance at vendors who promise to look the other way and merely give sly grins about your use of the outdated product.

If you lease the product, it is only yours as long as you pay the annual fee. In a rough budget year, if your funds are frozen early and you cannot pay the next year's bill, you must send all of the CD-ROM disks back. This is an important point, because there is little or no price difference between buying and leasing. Usually, buying is preferred unless leasing is required, because of copyright restrictions or other reasons.

What If I Have Trouble with Installation? Some vendors offer to come to your library, install the product, and provide you with training. If the source is online, certainly there should be some assistance with dial-in and modem set-up problems. The local representative will probably be doing this work, so be sure to ask how well trained that individual is. It would be helpful to have a customer service number available, preferably an 800 number that is in operation during the hours your library is open.

OTHER POINTS TO CONSIDER

Some CD-ROM vendors include the full text of a few magazine titles. This can be extremely helpful in several ways. A library can reduce its periodical budget if these magazines are used solely for research and are not browsing magazines. It is also helpful if the library does not receive those magazines and has no back issues.

On the down side, printing a list of citations is much faster than printing three or four full-text articles. A library media specialist must weigh the ability to print entire articles from the full-text magazines against the extra time that one patron will be using the CD-ROM product, preventing other patrons from using it.

Printing the full text also means that patrons will use fewer articles. With citations only, a patron may print out twenty citations and actually look up five or so of the articles. Printing out full-text articles is much slower and takes up a great deal of paper. Patrons will most likely print only two or three articles. One of the greatest benefits of an electronic magazine index is that patrons use a wider variety of magazine sources and increase the amount of reading that goes into the research-paper preparation. Using a full-text product may erase that benefit.

The product should be able to do some form of Boolean searching and offer users a symbol for truncation.

Some vendors provide posters, templates, and other printed material to display on or near the computer for the user's assistance. These should be easy to understand and easy to read from a distance. For additional help, the user's manual should have a thorough index and include illustrations of the screen choices. One way to evaluate the manual is to look up a term discussed in this article, such as "Boolean" or "truncation," to see how well it is explained. A glossary of terms is helpful also.

SET-UP

Electronic products offer varying degrees of local control or customization. Some allow the library media specialist to enter local comments on each record, to designate which magazines the library owns, and to limit the magazines found to that library's holdings. Judge these features in terms of their usefulness. What librarian really has time to enter comments into tens of thousands of records?

Moreover, limiting the records to local holdings may reduce the cost-effectiveness of the product. Instead of searching 100 magazine titles, now the user may be searching only 40 or 50. If a patron is using an electronic source and sees a citation for a magazine that your library does not have, it increases the chance that he or she may use another library or use interlibrary loan to retrieve that source.

The choice to limit searches to local holdings comes down to the size of the library's holdings and the ease of interlibrary loan. If one goal of the library is to encourage patrons to use the library as an "electronic doorway" to information in other libraries and sources, then limiting searches to local holdings would be counterproductive. If, however, there is only a limited interlibrary loan program and the size of the holdings meets most or all of the patron's needs, then perhaps limiting is a good choice.

The inconsistency of supporting a technology to create access to materials beyond the walls of the library and then altering the technology to limit the access to within the those walls must be given some consideration. The product may keep statistics on use, the number of hits for each title, and so forth. These features can be of value; however, the choice of a product should not hinge on them.

Command Searching

Some products allow the user to break out of the menu mode entirely and search the product by commands. Although this feature is only for experienced searchers, it does not take long for a user with aptitude to gain that experience, and many will welcome the ability to do this. This method is very similar to online searching; this way, users can practice such searching without racking up expensive online time.

Price

Some products offer staggered pricing according to how many times each year you would like updates. A library may opt to get them monthly, quarterly, or annually. There are additional search modes available with some vendors. The ability to log on to the vendor's online database for free with the purchase of the

CD-ROM subscription is one offer that is well worthwhile. A vendor may also offer a discount to educational institutions.

CONCLUSION

Basically, what librarians need from a magazine index on CD-ROM is for patrons to be able to use the product with very little assistance, print their citations as quickly as possible, and then move off the computer to allow other patrons to search. Any feature beyond the basic ones is of fairly limited usefulness.

The most important feature to you is the speed of the total search process, not just how quickly the computer finds the topic after if is entered. The key factor is how much time each patron will be occupying the computer.

As you evaluate the product, you must decide its features are really of value to the research process. Also decide whether each particular feature will increase or decrease the amount of time one patron spends at the computer performing a search.

The impact of an electronic magazine index on a library program is tremendous. The old requirement in many high school libraries of three magazine sources per term paper will become extinct, because students will use many more than that. For most libraries, this will become a purchase they will not regret.

7

Other Electronic Resources

Just about any library, large or small, will need to have an encyclopedia and magazine index in electronic form. These two resources will cover the great majority of reference and research questions from patrons. In some ways, the purchase decisions relating to these two types of resources are relatively easy to make, because the field is fairly limited in each category, and the purpose and use of these types of resources is roughly the same in all libraries.

After these purchase decisions are made, however, the library must decide what other kinds of resources should be obtained. How many and what type of electronic resources a library should offer is difficult to say for sure. It depends not only on the size of the library but more importantly on the goals of the program and the needs of the users. Choosing to offer the greatest possible number and variety of resources is not always wise, especially when one considers the cost of some products. Even the most inexpensive electronic resource is likely to be costlier than the most expensive reference book. When making a decision on which electronic resources should be added to complete the collection, think of this comparison.

Another criterion to ponder is the number of resources that can be used at the same time and on the same computer. It may be helpful to the library program to have the encyclopedia and magazine index up and running for a period of time before adding other resources. This way, the amount of use these two resources receive can be measured. After six months, it should be obvious whether it will be possible to place another product on the system or whether more computers will have to be made available for use with other products.

The most efficient way to use an electronic resource is to have it networked so that it can be available to several patrons at the same time. Doing so helps to ensure that the resource can be used whenever a patron needs it. As discussed in an earlier chapter, networking means that software is placed on a central computer, which is connected to several workstations. Patrons can have access to the software at any of the workstations. Generally, this means that multiple patrons can use the product at the same time.

It is important to monitor how much a product is used, a task that can be done by simple observation. Some database products create a running search log; insofar as this does not invade the patron's right to privacy, such logs may be helpful in planning for future uses of the system.

A stand-alone workstation is an alternative to networking and is chosen by some libraries, especially in the beginning stages. Stand-alone workstations may receive more use from patrons; a product that is booted up in a computer is its own advertisement to patrons, especially if it has some sort of flashy opening screen or a poster tacked up beside it. A program that is listed as one of ten or so options on the menu of a networked computer may not be used as much, because all a patron will know about it is the title listed on the computer screen alongside all of the other titles.

Another advantage to a single workstation is that the library staff can monitor the use of the products by a glance from across the library. And if a patron returns to the reference desk with a question about how to use "that computer over there," the experienced reference librarian will know at once which product is being referred to.

The disadvantage of a stand-alone workstation is that only one patron can use the electronic resource at any one time. For the encyclopedia or magazine index, this can be a real problem. For other, less frequently used products, a stand-alone may in fact be preferable; the occasional patron who uses it will not be taking up a network terminal and hindering the majority from using other products.

It may also be wise to use the stand-alone workstation to try out new products. Sometimes patron input as to whether or not a product should be purchased is very helpful, and a workstation next to the reference desk may help library staff with the initial questions that inevitably come with newly added products. Once the same question has been answered 15 or more times in a day, it may be obvious that some signage is necessary near the workstation.

WHAT TO BUY

Electronic resources come in many formats, and choosing which format to buy is difficult. Generally, hard-disk-resident databases, which can be loaded in their entirety onto one or more computers, provide the fastest access (keeping in mind that the speed of the computer is a factor also). The only limitation to placing more and more databases on the hard drive is the size of the drive itself. It is sometimes cost-efficient to purchase more memory or even buy a computer with the biggest possible hard drive your budget will allow in order to accommodate a greater number of databases. Besides the speed of the search itself, you can enter and exit a hard-disk-resident database much more quickly than a CD-ROM or online database.

When selecting electronic resources, do not overlook small hard-disk-resident databases. Many times the products can be networked along with the other electronic resources and add finishing touches to a well-rounded electronic information program. Remember that when patrons see a list of 10 choices on a computer menu, they do not care what the format is, indeed will probably not even *know* what the format is. Their only consideration will be whether or not a database fills their information needs.

Online resources can also be added to an electronic information program with relative ease. Because these resources are only dialed into when needed, there is no size limitation, as there is with hard-disk-resident databases or CD-ROMs. There is however, a mental limitation. Because online services charge by the minute, the librarian needs to be skilled in the use so as to minimize the time spent online. It is difficult to maintain any sort of skill level for more than about three different online services, because each has its own commands and database structure.

There are literally hundreds of electronic products to choose from, and deciding which are best for your program is extremely difficult. Price is not the only consideration; it is better to have a few resources that are useful than dozens of products that are rarely if ever used. Whereas the encyclopedia and magazine indexes serve a variety of purposes, other products could be used for quick reference questions, in-depth research, or other, more specialized purposes. The main question that should be answered is: What will this product do that either cannot be done with existing resources or cannot be done as efficiently with existing resources?

WHAT CAN IT DO?

An electronic resource should have multiple indexes, so that information can be researched in several ways. When you are considering a new product, sketch out the fields that make up the database. Then, when evaluating the product, see how many of those fields are indexed. It is surprising that some products offer only slightly better access in electronic form than their print versions do. There is little advantage to purchasing such products.

The more fields that are indexed, the better the access to the information. Certainly Boolean searching should be available, along with some sort of full-text searching. The size of the indexes may be very large, but if virtually every word in an encyclopedia can be indexed, then certainly other products with fewer words can be indexed also.

Variable printout capabilities also exist. If the text contains data that could conceivably be in chart form, then the product should allow the chart or table to be printed.

The question you should constantly ask is: What *should* the product be able to do? Then match that list against what the product actually *does*. It would be nice if the product can do more than you thought it could; if not, weigh the discrepancy against the cost of the product to see if it really is worth the price or if the print version can meet most patron needs.

Matching the Resource
to the Program

An electronic encyclopedia and magazine index will be used by the entire population of the library at one time or another. It is possible that, in fact, *every* person doing research would find it beneficial to use one or both of these resources. So when making the purchase decision for those resources, depth and breadth of coverage for a wide range of subjects is desirable.

When adding resources beyond those two initial purchases, a librarian may well consider using the opposite criteria and purchase a program that is only targeted to a small portion of the population or that fits a very specific need in the curriculum. How many general resources can a patron use before moving on to more specific ones? The answer to that may well be one or two.

Searching for products that fit a specific niche in the curriculum does have its dangers, however. Most librarians with experience in the electronic market-place can tell of purchasing a wonderful product with tremendous and fantastic capabilities and great value. The only problem was that it was not used or was only used to a fraction of its full potential. When searching for the niche products, do not let the dazzling technology keep you from considering how the product will fit into the library program.

It is a given that the product should meet all of the general criteria mentioned in chapter 3. Beyond that, there are other questions to be considered before adding a program to a library.

Is There a Need for the
Content of the Resource?

The technology of electronic information resources is truly fascinating. Librarians who remember patrons' struggles to use print products will be tremen-dously excited with new search technologies. What a product can do is very important, but there will have to be a reason for the patron to use it. Sometimes it helps to compare an electronic product to a reference book and consider how much of the library's print collection covers that topic.

There is such a thing as too much information. Even a patron doing specific research on a topic will not want everything ever printed about that topic. Be careful with information overload as you are searching for products.

In their sales spiels, vendors commonly refer to the cents per record. Even though one product may be $1,000 or so more expensive than another, the sales people will tell you with great pride that it is actually cheaper because there is a savings of 20 cents per record. Such claims should be given very little weight. Remember that the total cost of the product is what you will have to defend in a budget presentation, not the cents per record. The higher cost must be justified by the additional information provided. If the extra information is necessary in order to satisfy patron needs, then it may be worth paying a little extra.

Sometimes, however, the additional information is of dubious worth. There are electronic products that have in-depth geographic information on every state, including just about every statistic that has ever been collected on a wide range of topics. For people who need statistics on how their state corresponds to other states, such data are invaluable. However, is there a need for that depth of information in the library, or do the standard references fit most patrons' needs? Ask yourself this question: If this resource were in place during the last year, how many times would you have directed patrons to it to locate information that could not be found elsewhere? If the answer to that question is few or none, do not automatically discount the purchase. Consider the follow-up question: How many times would you have directed patrons to use the resource, even though they could find the same information elsewhere, because they could find the information *better* and *faster* in the electronic form? Computers do not make people lazy; they make them more efficient. A library that denies the most efficient access to information possible through technology will have difficulty justifying its importance to its community.

OTHER QUESTIONS

Another factor to be considered is the number of workstations that patrons have to choose from. In a library with an automated catalog, electronic encyclopedia, and electronic magazine index, most of the workstations in use at any given time will be running one of those three programs. If a library has a lot of general resources that may be used by most patrons, a great deal of time may be spent waiting for the computer to exit one product and load another. Therefore, it may be wise to concentrate on more specific products. However, if a library chooses to purchase multiple electronic products of generally the same type (such as various types of electronic encyclopedias), the number of workstations will have to be increased so that more patrons can use these products. Another solution may be to simply designate certain stations that will always be used for certain products.

When electronic resources were first introduced in libraries, it was common (especially in school libraries) for patrons to have to prove to the librarian that all print sources were exhausted before being permitted to use the electronic source. This seems ridiculous now, yet it is essentially what libraries do when they do not purchase a resource that would make an information search more efficient. Therefore, another question to consider is whether there are research questions that patrons have not asked because the resource that would answer them most efficiently was not in place. "Serendipitous searching" refers to questions people invent because a new resource appears that sparks their interest and allows them to find answers easily. Some resources need some publicity and urging before their use is found. After an initial slow period, they will find their niche.

You might ask how this resource matches the interests of the patron population. It is not always possible to say for sure that a resource is better suited to a university or special library collection than a school or public library. If a public library is situated in a strong medical community, then perhaps there is a need for a research-level medical database. If a public or school library serves a farm-oriented community, then an agricultural database may be a wise purchase. It could be that there is no interest as yet in the purchase of such a database, but a proactive library will understand that service to a population means providing not only materials patrons want but also resources they need.

How Much Will This Actually Be Used?

It could be that the product will only be used during the spring semester, or in the summer, or at some other time. Just because the audience for the resource is limited, however, is not a reason to discount purchase. Certainly some of the library's print collection must be designated to serve a small percentage of the patron group with distinct and continuing needs. Therefore, some of the electronic resource program should also be thus developed.

In fact, sometimes it is easier to make a purchase decision for resources that are limited in use. It is then possible for users to schedule specific times to work with the resource. At other times, other resources can be placed in that computer.

If the answers to all the questions above still indicate that use will be too limited, then the purchase should probably not be made. Any librarian experienced in electronic resources can tell you of truly wonderful products that they own, products that can do the most amazing things, if only patrons would use them.

Just as with any other resource, selection criteria must include patrons' research interests and their use patterns with other electronic products, not just how truly incredible the technology of the product is. The danger is that a librarian experienced with electronic resources will find it difficult not to buy the latest toy that hits the market.

CONCLUSION

Rounding out the electronic resource collection is a never-ending task. Just as in a print collection, the selection process is always in progress. New resources must be carefully evaluated and added when their value to the library program is the greatest. It also could be that resources need to be discarded when their use no longer justifies their occupying scarce computer space or when the hardware can be better used for other purposes.

However, limited space should not be a reason for *not* buying an electronic resource. When a print collection outgrows the reference area, new shelves are purchased, and sometimes the entire area must be reconfigured in order to hold more resources and allow the maximum use by patrons. Very few librarians will decline to purchase a print resource because it will not fit on the shelf. In the same way, occasionally the electronic resources program must be reconfigured so that the most resources possible will be available to the patron population.

Selection of electronic resources is risk-taking behavior. There is always the chance that the wrong choice will be made. A decision may be made to purchase the best resource currently on the market on a given subject, even though there are inherent and obvious flaws in it. Immediately thereafter, a new product might arrive that is much better and has fewer (or no) flaws. There is no way to avoid such situations. Keeping the library program abreast with new technologies means that sometimes the wrong decision will be made. It is far better to make those wrong decisions and offer patrons at least some service than to wait for the ultimate, indisputably best product, which may arrive too late for patron needs.

8

Selection of
Online Resources

Instead of purchasing or leasing a database that will be stored on a CD or hard drive in the library, some libraries choose to dial in to the database via modem. These large databases are usually stored in huge mainframe computers that may be located literally anywhere in this country or elsewhere. These resources are referred to as *online* databases.

Almost every library needs to have access to online databases. There are far too many resources available in electronic form; a library can never purchase all the databases its patrons will ever need. Even if a library did have that enormous a budget, it is difficult to imagine the size of the computer that would be needed to store them all.

Both large and small libraries generally offer online services. The largest libraries, with many electronic resources, will offer some kind of online service for patrons whose needs are not met by the resources on hand. A small library, by contrast, may rely more heavily than a large institution on online services, because these resources can satisfy the occasional search request in a database that a larger library would find more cost-efficient to purchase. Online databases may be offered initially to see if the use warrants purchase of the electronic database.

There is a bewildering array of online resources available, and the cost varies wildly. Choosing the right service for your library and deciding how many services to offer can be difficult decisions to make.

SUPERMARKET VENDORS

Suppose your library offered perhaps 50 to 100 online databases, each with its own searching instructions and commands. Imagine how difficult it would be to learn the multitude of search languages, the scope of each of the databases, logon and logoff instructions, and so forth. Fortunately, it is not necessary to learn all these separate protocols; one online service can provide the library with several hundred databases at once.

These are referred to as "supermarket vendors"; like a supermarket, where one can pick and choose from a variety of products, these online services offer a great variety of databases. Patrons can dial into the service and, using a single set of search commands, use any of the databases offered.

Most libraries subscribe to one of these supermarket vendors. A library may offer more than one supermarket online service, but that rarely happens. Using online services is unique in that you truly do not pay for the service until you use it, and you only pay for what you use. In some cases, there is no annual fee or minimal charge. If a library only uses the service an hour a year, it will be charged only for that one hour of time spent online.

Because of the hourly fee structure, expert searchers try to spend as little time as possible online doing a search. They use software products and printed subject thesauri to complete their searches as quickly and with as few commands as possible. It is very difficult to become expert on two systems. Conducting an online search takes great concentration, and trying to keep straight two different searching structures would be confusing and distracting.

Using an Online Service

In order to adequately make a decision concerning an online service, it is necessary to have some understanding of a typical search process with an online database vendor. The search process can be broken down into the following steps: pre-search, logon, search, printing, and logoff.

Pre-Search. Most libraries have developed some sort of paper form to assist the patron in formulating the exact question to be answered by the online search. When a patron comes in with a request, the librarian will assist him or her in filling out this form. The librarian most likely will perform a reference interview and review existing print resources to make sure that no duplicate resources exist in the library.

Once it has been determined that an online search is indeed necessary, the librarian and patron will decide which databases will be searched, and the librarian will check the documentation on those databases to see if there are any special ways they can be searched that would aid this particular search request and make for a faster or more thorough search. If there is a printed list of subjects used in the database, that will also be checked for any exact matches in the subject headings.

Logon. After the search is planned thoroughly and there is a written search strategy, the librarian and patron are ready to actually begin the search. Just as home telephone users choose a long-distance service, online researchers choose a computer telecommunications network. Generally, each network has a local access number in most metropolitan areas of any size. If your area does not have one, there will be a long-distance charge to use the telecommunication network. It is not necessary to subscribe to the telecommunications network, merely to choose which network to use when logging on. The cost of using the telecommunications network will be part of the online fee.

In some libraries, the logon software is pre-set to automatically put in the user code, password, and correct telephone numbers. At others, the librarian will enter those items at the appropriate time during the logon procedure. Either option could be preferred for security reasons, and each individual library must choose the approach that best suits its own needs. If the computer used for online searching is in a secure area, where there is no chance that an adept user will be unsupervised while on the computer (and possibly rack up large online bills), then the library may well choose the pre-set option. This way, no user can watch the librarian type in the secret codes.

However, if the computer is regularly used for a number of purposes, it may not be such a good idea to have a pre-set option; a patron may stumble onto the program and inadvertently (or intentionally) log on. In any event, the password can be changed frequently so that the level of security remains high.

Search. Once the password has been entered, the clock starts ticking, so the faster the search can be done, the cheaper it will be. The steps to searching are: 1) designate the appropriate database; 2) enter the search strategy; 3) review results and modify strategy; and 4) print the results.

Usually the database is designated by a number or code, and with some services it is possible to search multiple databases at the same time. The search strategy is usually indicated by a series of commands (generally a series of simple statements) or one long and complicated command. Usually command statements are not too long, however, because one typing error in a long statement will render the entire thing worthless.

Some software programs allow the searcher to enter the appropriate commands and search terms ahead of time, so that as soon as the logon process is completed, the search will automatically begin. If the library does a great deal of online searching or is greatly concerned about cost, these software packages are well worth investigating.

After the initial search is completed, the list of "hits," or records found, must be reviewed, and the records to display or print must be chosen. With experience, a practiced eye can quickly scan the list of records found in the search and determine if the search needs to be revised or if the records found are indeed relevant to the search request.

It is a good idea to have a clock near the computer at eye level so that the time online can be monitored. Sometimes, with difficult searches, a great deal of time can elapse with the revision of the search process. Because of the concentration involved in the search process, the passage of the time can go unnoticed.

Printing. If the search is satisfactory, there are several options for viewing the results. They can be printed out on the attached printer, saved to disk and printed at a later time, or, in some cases, ordered online and sent electronically. When they are ordered online, the next time that you log on, the documents are waiting there for you.

With most databases, there is a per citation print charge, so the number of citations a patron wishes to print will be chosen carefully.

Logoff. After the search has been completed, the librarian then types a command to log off the system. Usually, the cost of the search is shown, along with the time spent online. This is helpful in keeping track of accumulated costs and databases used, information that can be used to identify resources not available in the library. Libraries that charge their patrons for online searches can use this record for that purpose.

Fee Structure

The advantage of using a supermarket vendor is that no matter what database you are using, the command structure remains the same. The fees, however, vary with each database. Some databases, especially those that are government-sponsored and in the public domain, are fairly inexpensive, perhaps as little as $60 an hour. Others, such as scientific or medical databases, may be as much as $400 or more per hour.

Along with the database charge, there is a charge for the use of the online network that is used to connect your computer to the online vendor's computer. This telecommunications charge is added to the online cost charged by the online vendor. A typical telecommunications charge is $12 to $15 per hour.

The last charge is the citation print charge. The database documentation should list the different print formats that can be used, along with the cost of printing each. Some print formats are free, such as those that simply list the record number and title of the citation. These formats can be reviewed onscreen before printing.

One note to remember is that with online searching, "printing" can mean sending the citation to the printer, saving it to disk, or displaying it onscreen. The cost for each of these type of printing operations is the same.

In addition to the bill from the online searching vendor, the cost to the library in terms of staff time must be taken into consideration. It is not unusual for a librarian to spend several hours or more in preparation for an online search. Although there is usually no charge to the patron, it is a cost to the library and should be taken into account by those considering entering the online searching field.

With *purchased* databases such as CD-ROMs or hard-disk-resident pro-grams, one factor of cost-efficiency is the number of patrons who make use of the resource. Forcing patrons to use print resources as a prerequisite to using electronic resources simply does not make sense either logically or economically; the resources cost the same whether they are used constantly or not at all. However, because of the cost and fee structure of online searching, most libraries will insist that patrons first refer to print resources, then to any purchased databases the library may have, in search of the information they need. If these resources fail to yield the desired results, then online searching will be permitted.

Training

Most libraries will have a staff person trained to do online searches, and very few will allow patrons to use online services without any supervision. The cost of training, and the cost of the learning curve until the librarian becomes expert, must be taken into consideration for the first year at least.

Most online vendors hold full-day and half-day training and update sessions at locations around the country. These sessions provide the librarian with a basic understanding of search commands and logon procedures. Usually, the attendees are given passwords to a select number of free, small training databases where they can practice their skills.

Still, there is no substitute for regular searching to upgrade skills. This is why a relatively small number of library employees, rather than the entire staff, should be designated expert online searchers.

CRITERIA
FOR SELECTION

Supermarket vendors have the distinct advantage of having many databases and the convenience of one monthly charge instead of hundreds of small bills. Regular training sessions from the vendor, along with update sessions with some individual database producers, help users maintain a high skill level and learn tips to lower the cost of online searching.

Because vendors are rather similar in their approach to online searching, the criteria for selection may be more subtle in this area than in others. Here are a few questions to consider when making a decision about which online vendor to use.

Number and Kinds of Databases

Although the major online vendors offer roughly the same number and kinds of databases, there are some differences. The number of databases offered is not necessarily of concern; even libraries who have offered online searching for 20 years have not used all, or even most, of the databases offered. More important is the match between the types of the databases offered and the interests of the patrons in your particular library. A library that serves a scientific or medical community obviously will not choose databases with a humanities focus.

Along with the content of the databases, the intellectual and reading level of the material in the databases will be of some interest. In most cases, the databases are organized by the most advanced people in the field. Although some material may be understood by an upper-level elementary student, most material will be far above that level. This is not a reason to be discouraged in the selection of an online database; rather, it is simply another criterion to be aware of in the selection process. These differences among the major online vendors are subtle, but they are still worth at least some consideration.

Special Search Features

Ask about special features that make searching easier. Judge them on the same criteria you applied to the gadgetry features on CD-ROM products. Are they really useful, or are they features you will rarely use?

The ability to search several databases at the same time is an example of such a special feature. Although it is a useful feature, it is not always applicable. It is most useful when the databases to be searched are similar in content—two or three medical databases, for example. But suppose a search involved the topic of school libraries. The most pertinent resources are databases with information on education and those with information on libraries. However, multiple-file searching is not possible because the same search strategy cannot be used. In an education database, the searcher would look for "libraries," because searching for the word "school" in an education database would find practically every record. In the same way, one would not use the word "library" as part of the search term in a library database. Multi-database searching is a good feature to have at times, but it can only be used when the search words are going to be the same in each database. Each library will have to make its own judgment about the number of times that will occur. The above scenario is an example of the impracticality of some features. Use the same logic to think through some of the other wonderful features that you will be shown.

Another question should be asked of each feature is: Will it speed up or slow down the search process? If using the feature means that you will be spending more time online, then you will be spending more money. That will have to be balanced against whether or not the feature enables the patron to get a more complete search. Hopefully, the added cost will be well worth the increased value of the search to the patron.

Documentation
and Training

You should ask to see the written descriptions of the databases and any documentation the vendor deems helpful for the search. The descriptions of each database should be concise but complete. Sample searches are helpful, as are sample printouts, with which you can judge the intellectual and reading level of the database. Sometimes there are additional indexes that can be searched, and these should be listed as well. Some of the documentation will be free, and others will require a small charge. If your library is on a very tight budget, you may have to consider the costs of the documentation that you find most helpful.

Review the training offered by the vendors within the last year. Costs will be rather similar among vendors, but remember that you have to send someone to the training site. If you are fortunate there will be a training site within easy driving distance of your library so you will not have to pay for travel and an overnight stay. Check with the vendor to see who the trainer will be. There should be someone assigned to a regional area, so you will become familiar with the trainer over a period of time.

Costs

Costs are relatively similar among vendors, but there are some differences. Try picking several databases that you could visualize using fairly often and see what the cost would be for a five-minute search in each, assuming you printed out, say, 10 citations in each database. Also check to see if you need to use a long-distance line to make the call or if there is a local node in your area.

Some online vendors provide a greatly reduced searching rate for those teaching online search methods in a classroom setting. This discount can be of great benefit. Institutions must be very careful to use that rate only when teaching patrons; another rate must be specified for general use. With the reduced rate, the number of databases available for searching is also reduced.

The classroom rate is generally used for library schools and in elementary and secondary education. This is an additional service, and the complete vendor will offer teaching guides and documentation explaining the alternative search strategies and commands. Generally, the institutions eligible for the reduced rate will also have a regular password to be used when the reduced rate does not apply. Ask the vendor for the complete restrictions on the use of the classroom rate to see if they apply to your intended use of online searching.

Regional Preference

Call neighboring libraries that offer online searching and ask which vendor they are using. Especially if you are a one- or two-professional library, it is helpful if you can call a nearby librarian for assistance, and doing so is easier if both libraries are using the same database vendor.

OTHER ONLINE SERVICES

Occasionally the online user will hear of online databases other than those offered by supermarket vendors. Usually the user must dial the long-distance number to connect with the computer in which the database resides and pay the long-distance charges. The databases themselves are usually free. The NASA Space Database is an example of this type of service, and the information it contains is very helpful to aerospace clubs and those involved in education.

College and university library catalogs are also in this category. If a nearby college or university has an online public access catalog (OPAC), it is sometimes possible to dial in from a remote site (such as *your* library). Although some restrictions usually do apply, it is still a useful tool; you can log on and look at that library's collection to find out what is available before sending patrons there. This practice can be most helpful in easing the interlibrary loan load. If a great many periodicals are needed that are not held in your library, sometimes you can dial in to the local university library's catalog and see what periodical titles are held. Most university libraries are quite willing to serve the community, but it is always a good idea to contact that library's staff to check on their procedures. Sometimes this will be a local call for your computer and as such will cost almost nothing, but at other times a long-distance charge will be needed. Telephone charges are usually fairly inexpensive considering the length of time that can be spent online and the information that can be retrieved. It is possible to get some idea of the expense by contacting the telephone company and getting an estimate. It is also possible to search during non-peak hours for a reduced charge.

Consumer Online Services

An interesting development in electronic resources is the home market for electronic databases. Services such as Prodigy, CompuServe, and others are pitched to consumers on TV and in magazines. Because these services are relatively inexpensive and are usually easy to use, some libraries have chosen to install these products.

The criteria for choosing a consumer online service must be the same as choosing any other reference source. Specific criteria may include the speed of the product, which is especially true if many of the screens have graphics. The following questions are a quick guide.

What is the true reference value of the product? Some products claim to have reference databases such as encyclopedias, but in truth, the encyclopedias are not searchable by keyword access, only by title. It makes a tremendous difference if the highly touted newspaper database only contains current news, and then only a few selected columns.

How will the product be used? Will patrons search it for their information needs, or is the main purpose of the product electronic mail and bulletin boards? How fast is the product accessed, and would it be possible for a patron to unintentionally wander into a database that may be quite expensive, therefore costing the library big bucks in online time?

Is there another reason to buy the product? Even if a review of the product reveals that it is not a solid reference tool, some libraries may feel that they can serve a need in the community by purchasing the software and allowing patrons to access the service using their own ID and password.

A Word About Internet

A chapter on online services will not be complete without some mention of the Internet (although this is discussed in more detail in chapter 9). The Internet can be thought of as a superhighway of computer networks. It is not an entity in itself but rather a collection of networks that are interconnected, in much the same way roads intersect. Because some of the databases that libraries have previously purchased or leased are available in some parts of the Internet, it may be possible for a library to offer an incredible variety of databases to its experienced patrons.

Even more interesting is that if an institution offers the use of the Internet, each user can sign on individually. This means that the users will be using databases, retrieving documents, and using electronic mail without ever using any part of the library itself.

The mix and match of library-owned and online resources combine to provide endless variety for an electronic information resources program. Using online services to supplement other electronic information and explore new types of resources will provide the maximum benefits to patrons and allow for the most efficient use of time and money.

9

Internet

One of the more fascinating developments in recent years has been the development of an interconnected computer network called the Internet. Librarians in even the smallest libraries in the most remote areas should begin to read and become informed about the Internet. Eventually, the use of this computer network system will affect the way libraries provide services to patrons and to each other. In fact, Internet access is not uncommon in many libraries.

The Internet is not simply a computer network. Rather, it is an interconnection between various computer networks. The work that is being done to develop NREN—the National Research and Education Network—involves the same collection of networks.

UNDERSTANDING
THE CONCEPT

The easiest way to begin to understand the Internet is to think of the system of interstate highways. If you are planning a trip that begins at your front door, you will need to start with a local road, which will perhaps connect to a different road, which will then connect to an interstate highway. At the end of your journey, you would exit the interstate to a local road, then another local road, until you reached your destination. At some time during your journey you may have changed interstates, perhaps even several times.

The rules that governed your trip changed along the way. Perhaps the speed limit changed, or you reached a no-passing zone. You may have noticed a difference in the quality of the road. Sometimes traffic flowed unimpeded, and sometimes you may have been stopped completely in a traffic jam.

Using the Internet is similar to driving on the interstate: It is a way to travel from one place to another. Usually, the first step is to obtain some sort of password to a local computer network. From there, you will be able to reach another network through what are called *gateways* and continue on. Gateways are junctions that provide an "exit ramp" to another network.

The most experienced Internet users reach people around the world and use databases of incredible scope and size. Learning what is available and what services make sense for each library is not an easy or a fast process, and it has a lot to do with trial and error.

Learning about the Internet is a little bit like moving to a foreign language and trying to learn the language. At first, you understand nothing; then you might begin to understand unconnected phrases and words. Finally, it all starts to make a little bit of sense, even though as soon as you begin to talk you give yourself away as a novice.

Probably the way to begin to learn about the Internet is to read some articles about it. It is wisest to skim these, because you will probably not understand much. At local, state, and national conferences, programs are sometimes presented that may give an aspect of the use of the Internet. These can be very helpful, because they will both give you an idea of the kinds of uses available and help you identify experienced Internet users in your area who can be used as resources.

USES OF THE INTERNET

The use of the Internet can be divided into three main types: e-mail (Electronic Mail Communication), Telnet (Telecommunicating Network), and File Transfer Protocol (FTP). These categories will be referred to often as you learn the language of the Internet.

E-Mail

One of the most popular features of any computer network is the ability to contact people in other parts of the country or the world and have discussions at relatively little charge. Electronic mail communications are becoming extremely popular, and colleagues around the world can be in continual contact and hold forth on any variety of subjects.

Connecting via electronic mail can be very simple. As with the regular mail system, you need to know the name and address of the person to whom you are sending a message. On most Internet networks, the addresses are in two parts. The first part of the address is called the *ID* and is usually a combination of letters in the person's name. The ID of Barbara Jones, for example, might be BJONES.

The second part of the address is the *node* and is followed by an @ symbol. The node is the large mainframe or miniframe computer through which you are connecting to the electronic mail network. Most of these nodes are available through large colleges or universities, although certainly there are other institutions that have large computers.

On some smaller networks, it is possible to search for a person's e-mail address, but this is not really feasible on the larger networks. By far the easiest way to find someone's ID and node is to call them on the telephone and ask them.

There are two main ways to communicate with someone electronically. The most common is very similar to sending a letter through the post office. You address the message, type in the text, and then direct the computer to send. The message goes into the recipient's "mailbox" at the large mainframe or miniframe computer they log on to, and it waits there until they log on. When they do, a message usually appears on their computer screen to let them know they have mail waiting.

The other type of message, sometimes called a "chat" or "interactive e-mail," is similar to a telephone conversation. If both you and the intended recipient are online, you can send a short message, usually one line long, and it will instantaneously flash on that person's screen. The recipient can then respond directly, and the two of you can go back and forth, "talking" to each other in real time. This type of e-mail is rarely used, because when you log on you have no way of knowing if the person you want to talk to is logged on also. It is best to schedule this kind of communication in advance.

To a new user, eager to communicate electronically, finding someone to exchange e-mail with can be both exciting and frustrating. It is sort of like having one of the first telephones, and not knowing anyone to call.

A by-product of e-mail is the "bulletin board" service. These are called *listservs* and are one of the most popular uses of the Internet. Bulletin boards are generally tied to a single theme, and the electronic messages sent there can be read by anyone who logs on. Depending on the size of the service, a message may reach thousands of people at once. There are listservs established for libraries (e.g., music librarians or bibliographic instruction) and for people who share a certain reading interest (e.g., horror) or other recreational interest.

Several words of caution about listservs. The concept of communicating electronically with thousands of colleagues, all with common interests, is truly exciting. The novice user is tempted to spend several hours reviewing the hundreds and hundreds of listservs available and joining all that even remotely apply. Once you join a listserv, however, you will begin getting e-mail; you will begin getting *lots and lots* of e-mail. In fact, you could easily spend hours each day doing nothing but reading e-mail messages. Perhaps a better way to begin is by joining the one or two listservs that are most pertinent to your interests and seeing how much mail that generates.

There is a children's story titled "Pigs Is Pigs." This is the story of a follow-the-rules post office that insisted that guinea pigs were domestic animals and should be charged at the domestic animals rate. The person mailing the two pigs maintained that guinea pigs were pets and should be mailed at a cheaper rate. As the conversation deteriorated, the guinea pigs were left at the office until a decision from on high was reached. Needless to say, the guinea pigs multiplied until, at the end of the story, with thousands and thousands of guinea pigs, the harried post office gladly mailed them all at the lower rate. This is exactly what can happen to a person who innocently joins a listserv. The first day, you might have thirty messages. Wow, you think, and you check about half of them. The next day you are busy and do not check it at all. The next day, when you log on, you have 150 messages waiting for you. Totally undone by that amount, you check a few and log off. Maybe a week later, when you gather courage, you find there are close to 1,000 messages. An embarrassing point of this story is that, if you have the Internet account through your institution, you usually are allocated only so much disk space. You may receive an admonishing call from the system administrator warning you that you have exceeded your allotted space.

When a bulletin board message is read, it can be replied to on the screen. Sometimes it is easy to forget that the reply will go out as another bulletin board message, where thousands of users may read it. If your reply is not meant for everyone to see, you can respond privately to the sender by forwarding the message to that person's e-mail address.

Vacation time presents another reminder to the Internet user. Most mainframes denote a specific amount of space in the computer for each user. Usually there is no danger of filling up that space as long as you read and discard your mail on a regular basis. But when you are out of the office for several days or weeks, unread mail may pile up and fill the allotted space. For those times, it is possible to turn the mail off; the listserv operator will temporarily delete you from the list so that you will not be receiving any mail. Then when you return to the daily routine, it is a simple matter to turn the mail back on again.

Telnet

Through Telnet, it is possible to reach other private databases (such as university library catalogs) or public domain databases (such as ERIC). Some of these databases may in fact be similar to ones that your library has been paying a fee to purchase or lease.

The number and type of databases available is mind-boggling. Hundreds of major university library catalogs are listed, and it is just as easy to search the catalog of a library across the country as it is to search one that may be across town. Fees are required to search some databases. Whether it is more cost-efficient to search the database on the Internet or purchase, lease, or log on to the database through more conventional methods is something that the individual library will have to decide.

File Transfer Protocol

File Transfer Protocol (FTP) is an advanced feature of the Internet that makes it possible to send files of data to others on the computer network. It is also possible to retrieve data from the Internet. For example, users can search databases and locate statistics or even the entire text of journal articles, then download the information directly into their own computers. This is a use that will have great value to expert users but only limited value to novices.

GAINING ACCESS TO
THE INTERNET

Because the Internet is simply a connection of networks, you cannot have a password directly to it. Access is obtained by subscribing to a computer system that is connected to the Internet. The cost of the Internet will depend on the cost of the computer network. There may also be a long-distance charge to log on to the nearest node.

If you are considering subscribing to an electronic mail network, ask if there is a connection to the Internet. Do not be swayed if you are given promises that access will be available in "two months" or "by October." Software that is promised to be available in just a short time is referred to as "vaporware," because it is sometimes little more than air. It may be wise to choose a service that currently offers Internet access. Whether you just use the Internet yourself on a professional level or allow patrons to use it as well will depend on your level of confidence in the sophistication of the general library population.

Your institution may have access to the Internet through an internal e-mail service that makes use of the institution's mainframe or miniframe computer. Check with the computer services branch of your institution for more information.

IMPACT
OF THE INTERNET

The impact of the Internet on library service is just beginning to be discussed. The idea that Internet users are able to search databases, download data, and perhaps even retrieve full-text copies of journal articles without ever setting foot in a library can be unsettling. Certainly libraries will have to come to terms with the possibilities of the Internet in order to remain in the forefront of information service in the new millennium.

If someone unfamiliar with the Internet asks a more experienced user, "Just what is on the Internet?" the question is usually met with a sigh and a one-word answer: "Lots." There is so much information available that it is difficult to even describe the Internet, let alone become adept at using it. There are several published handbooks on the subject, and it might be wise for the beginning user to read one or more of these. As you make your way around the Internet, there are some opening direction screens that can be printed and saved. There are also some handbooks available in electronic form on the Internet, and printing these as you find them may also be helpful.

There is no library so small that it can ignore the impact of the Internet on the future of library services. Regardless of whether or not it is possible for your library to have access now, it is wise to begin the learning process by reading and attending workshops on the Internet, so that when you do have access you will be able to make better use of the services available.

10

What the
Future Holds

The one thing a librarian with any experience in electronic information sources will tell you is that the program is never finished. There is never a time to sit back and look with satisfaction at a job well done. At each juncture, there is another new program on the market that threatens to make the previous one obsolete.

The fear of wasting the institution's money on a course of action that may well become obsolete before completion is even reached may make some librarians hesitate before entering the electronic information age. This is certainly cause for concern, but it is impossible for a library to provide even adequate service unless some form of electronic information is provided.

Most library programs will contain a mix of information. Certainly the library catalog will be automated, although some will be more concerned with providing electronic journal access than with automating a catalog that exists in print form. Access to some databases that are too large to exist on a library microcomputer and therefore must be purchased in CD form or offered online give the library user a concept of the depth and breadth of information available in today's world.

Once a library has started down the path to the electronic information age, it is difficult to slow down the process. Some staff time must be devoted to staying up to date with new resources and seeking new cost-efficient ways of providing information to patrons. Apart from regularly attending library conferences and networking with other professionals in similar situations, reading the literature can be extremely helpful in this regard. Within the last few years, several library periodicals have established regular columns dealing with the selection of electronic resources. Although coverage is better in the more established columns, sometimes reviewers still fall into the trap of reviewing the *technology* rather than the use of the product in the library program. It is not uncommon for a reviewer to give a negative evaluation to an electronic source on the basis of the difficulty of installation. That is similar to a book reviewer advising that a book purchase be passed up because the source may be difficult to shelve.

There are periodicals specifically written to the various electronic formats. These, too, tend to focus on the technology, although certainly that has been improving also.

The best way to decide which journals to read is to ask for sample issues, then compare them to find your best choice. Criteria for the selection of the journal may well hinge on the degree to which technical information is emphasized. A novice in electronic information sources may be lost in some of the more technical journals, whereas a more experienced user may crave that aspect. A thorough perusal of sample issues will help make this decision a lot easier.

A VIEW OF THE FUTURE

Where the electronic information field is eventually heading is difficult to foresee. Certainly, information is growing at an alarming rate, even as the amount of information we can absorb at one time seems to be decreasing. Already, school libraries are beginning to teach the use of electronic resources early in the elementary grades. The expectations these children have of public and university libraries when they reach adulthood will be very high.

We are definitely in the midst of an information age, and we are finding that information on a computer screen. Library patrons will either look to us to lead the way in providing access to information or look away from us and find the information themselves.

GLOSSARY

A/B switch   Inexpensive small box that can be used to connect one peripheral to two different computers. For example, one printer can be shared between two computers by the use of an A/B switch box. When the dial is turned to Computer A, Computer A can print; when turned to B, Computer B can print.

Baud   Bits per second. Used to describe the speed of a computer modem.

bibliographic database   A database consisting of bibliographic citations, such as a magazine index. *See also* database.

browse mode   The mode of searching that matches the search word against an alphabetic list of subjects or titles.

Boolean searching   The use of the *and*, *or*, and *not* connectors to expand the searching capability of an electronic resource product.

CD-ROM (compact disk-read only memory)   a laser-encoded disk with information that is read in a CD-ROM player.

command line   A line of print at the very top or very bottom of the screen that gives the user information about the program or database.

CPU   Central Processing Unit. The main processor of a computer. *See also* processor.

database   A collection of information, usually on a specific topic, that can be separated in distinct parts. *See also* bibliographic database; directory database; field; full-text database; numeric database; and record.

directory database   A database that contains lists of information, similar to a telephone book. *See also* database.

documentation   The manual or guide that accompanies an electronic product and contains the instructions for the use of the product.

electronic resources   Any information that can be accessed through a computer. The information may be contained in the computer or a CD-ROM drive, or it may be accessed through a modem and telephone line from a distant location.

embedded truncation   A symbol used in the middle of a word that can substitute for any letter. Example: Wom#n. *See also* truncation.

field   A separate, identifiable part of a database record. *See also* database; record.

floppy disk   A storage or program disk inserted in the computer during use. Floppy disks come in two sizes: 5¼ inch and 3½ inch. The 3½-inch disk is enclosed in a hard plastic cover, but it is still a floppy disk.

front-end software   The searching software, usually loaded on the hard drive of the computer, used to retrieve data stored on another device such as a CD-ROM disk. Also called search engine.

full-text   A record that contains the full text of a particular document.

full-text database   A database with records that contain the complete text of a publication. *See also* database.

hard disk   An internal information storage device on a computer.

hit   A search result in which the search words were found in the database.

input   The command or keys used by the user.

keyword searching   Refers to the ability of the computer to search any word in a database field. *See also* word search.

logon   Connecting into a database or network, usually through a modem and telephone line.

mainframe   An extremely large computer.

megabyte   1,024 bytes. Used to measure the amount of data or data storage. On most home computers, hard disks are 30–40 megabytes.

miniframe computer   A smaller version of a mainframe computer.

modem   The connection device between the computer and the telephone line that allows the user to do online searching.

monitor The screen of the computer. Can also refer to the type of television screen that can be connected to a computer.

monochrome A non-color monitor.

network A connection made between two computers so that each can use the same software or program at the same time.

non-print The collection of audio-visual material in a library. It is also used to describe materials other than the usual books, journals, and text materials.

numeric database A database containing mostly numeric data, such as stock quotations. *See also* database.

online searching Logging on to a remote database, usually stored in a mainframe computer.

output Removing data from a computer, either by printing it on a printer or saving it on a floppy disk.

peripherals Extra accessories for a computer, such as a modem or mouse.

print Traditional textual materials such as books or journals.

processor The central working unit of a computer; determines the computer's power. Most IBM-compatible home computers now have 386 or 486 processors. *See also* CPU.

projection panel A large-screen projection device that rests on the top of an overhead projector and projects the image on the computer monitor onto a screen.

proximity operators Commands or symbols that tell the computer how close together the search words must be.

pull-down windows Overlays of possible commands that are pulled down by a keystroke or command of the user.

RAM random access memory, refers to the space that can be taken up by a program. Also refers to the amount of space a program needs in order to run.

record A complete set of information held in a database. *See also* database; field.

search engine *See* front-end software.

setup   The initial organization of a program. During the setup mode, the user will tell the computer what printer is being used, which slot the modem is in, and other such information.

slots   In order to add peripherals to a computer, circuitry cards for each peripheral must be inserted in slots, located inside the processor.

stand-alone   A computer not connected to any other in a network.

stop words   Words found in a database field too commonly to be indexed, such as *a*, *an*, or *the*.

terminal   One of the computers on a network. Also can be described as a "dumb terminal," since only one computer on a network needs to have a hard drive.

truncation   Shortening words to aid in searches. For example, truncating "library" by using "librar*" would yield the terms "libraries," "librarian(s)," "library," and so on. *See also* embedded truncation.

upgrade   A new version of a computer program.

videodisc   A laser-encoded disk containing mostly visual material, for instance, slides or moving pictures.

word search   The ability to search any word in a field. *See also* keyword searching.

workstation   A terminal or stand-alone computer; usually a complete computer set-up for a user, containing computer, any needed peripherals, and printer.

zero hits   A search result in which the search words were not found in the database.

Bibliography

Baumback, Donna J. "CD-ROM: Information at Your Fingertips." *School Library Media Quarterly*, Spring 1990, 42–49.

Bankhead, Betty. "Through the Technology Maze: Putting CD-ROM to Work." *School Library Journal*, October 1991, 44–49.

Bankhead, Elizabeth. "CD-ROM 1990-1992: A Selected Bibliography." *School Library Journal*, October 1991, 46–47.

Beiser, Karl. "Specs for a CD-ROM Workstation." *Online*, July 1993, 101–04.

Churbuck, David C. "The CD-ROM Survival Guide (CD-ROM Players)." *Forbes*, November 8, 1993, 320–21.

Civale, Cosmo. "Connecting Library and Classroom Environments Via Networking." *Media and Methods*, March/April 1991, 32–34.

Clark, Katie. "A Practical Commentary on the Selection of CD-ROM vs. Online Databases." *CD-ROM Professional*, July 1991, 115–16.

Davis, Trisha L. "Acquisition of CD-ROM Databases for Local Area Networks." *Journal of Academic Librarianship*, Vol. 19, No. 2 (May 1993), 68–71.

Denton, Barbara. "E-Mail Delivery of Search Results Via the Internet." *Online*, March 1992, 50–53.

Desmarais, Norman. *CD-ROM Local Area Networks: A User's Guide.* Westport, CT: Meckler, 1991.

Flanders, Bruce L. "Spinning the Hits: CD-ROM Networks in Libraries." *American Libraries*, December 1990, 1032–33.

Gielda, Scott A. "CD-ROM Drives: What's Available and What to Look for When Buying One." *Laserdisk Professional*, January 1989, 13–19.

Graham, John R. "Who Are Next Year's Customers?" *Supervision*, August 1993, 13–15.

Grossman, Becky Lockwood. "Buying Your Next CD-ROM Workstation? Some Practical Tips." *CD-ROM Professional*, March 1992, 33–36.

Haar, John, Juleigh Muirhead Clark, and Sally Jacobs. "Choosing CD-ROM Products." *College & Research Libraries News*, October 1990, 839–841.

Jaffe, Lee David, and Steven G. Watkins. "CD-ROM Hardware Configurations: Selection and Design." *CD-ROM Professional*, January 1992, 62–68.

Johnson, Denise. "CD-ROM Selection and Acquisition in a Network Environment." *Computers in Libraries*, October 1991, 17–22.

Kehoe, Brendan P. *Zen and the Art of the Internet: A Beginner's Guide.* 2d ed. New York: Prentice-Hall, 1993.

Kesselman, Martin A. "The Internet." *Wilson Library Bulletin*, March 1992, 78–80.

LaGuardia, Cheryl M. "Virtuous Disc Selection: Or, How I Learned to Stop Worrying and Love to Buy CD-ROMs." *CD-ROM Professional*, January 1992, 58–60.

Lane, Elizabeth, and Craig Summerhill. *Internet Primer for Information Professionals: A Basic Guide to Internet Networking Technology.* Westport, CT: Meckler, 1992.

Langlois, Jennifer. "CD-ROMs: Considerations Before Purchasing." *CD-ROM Librarian*, December 1990, 17–19.

————. "CD-ROMs: What to Consider Before Leasing or Purchasing." *Show-Me Libraries*, Fall 1990, 13–19.

Lathrop, Ann. *Online and CD-ROM Databases in School Libraries: Readings.* Englewood, CO: Libraries Unlimited, 1989.

Lynch, Daniel C., and Marshall T. Rose. *Internet System Handbook.* Redding, MA: Addison-Wesley, 1992.

Lyskowinski, Sharon. "Networking CD-ROM Workstations." *Media and Methods*, May/June 1991, 10.

McQueen, Howard. "Network CD-ROMs: Implementation Considerations." *Laserdisk Professional*, March 1990, 13–16.

Mendrinos, Roxanne. "A CD-ROM Network Allows Multiple Users to Simultaneously Access Discs." *Electronic Learning*, April 1990, 32–33.

Molettiere, Richard. "A Guide to Networking." *Media and Methods*, November/December 1991, 40–43+.

Nelson, Nancy Melin. "CD-ROM Growth: Unleashing the Potential." *Library Journal*, February 1, 1991, 5+.

———. "CD-ROM Roundup." *Library Journal*, February 1, 1990, 45–50.

Nicholls, Paul Travis. "CD-ROM in the Library: Implications, Issues and Sources." *Laserdisk Professional*, March 1990, 100–103.

———. "CD-ROM in the Schools: A Technology Overview and Bibliography." *Information Searcher* 3, No. 1, 1990, S-1.

Nickerson, Gord. "The CD-ROM Workstation: What It Is and What to Look For." *CD-ROM Professional*, September 1991, 81–85.

———. "Local Databases: Remote Access on the Internet to Locally Mounted Databases." *Computers in Libraries*, January 1992, 37–39.

———. "Networked Resources: Databases on the Internet." *Computers in Libraries*, December 1991, 38–42.

Nissley, Meta, and Nancy Melin Nelson. *CD-ROM Licensing and "Copyright Issues for Libraries."* Westport, CT/London: Meckler, 1990.

Polly, Jean Armour. "Surfing the Internet: An Introduction." *Wilson Library Bulletin*, June 1992, 38–42.

Quint, Barbara E. "Online Meets the Internet." *Wilson Library Bulletin*, March 1992, 78–80.

Reese, Jean. "CD-ROM Technology in Libraries: Implications and Considerations." *Electronic Library*, February 1990, 26–35.

Rieger, Oya Y. "Introducing Numeric CD-ROMs in Your Library: Challenges and Issues." *Microcomputers for Information Management*, Vol. 10, No. 2 (June 1993), 93–118.

Robinson, Carol. "Publishing's Electronic Future." *Publishers Weekly*, September 6, 1993, 46–48.

Rutherford, John. "Improving CD-ROM Management through Networking." *CD-ROM Professional*, September 1990, 20–27.

Index

A/B switches, 19-20
Abstracts, 59, 62
Anti-static pads, 22
Assessing needs, 38-39
Authoritativeness (selection
    criteria), 35

Bibliographic databases, 4-5
Bibliographic magazine, 58
Boolean operators, 50
Boolean searching, 29-30, 47, 64
Browse mode (in databases), 26-27,
    49-50, 61
Bulletin boards, 87
Buyer's remorse, 44
Buying versus leasing, 63-64

Cables, 19
CD encyclopedias, 45-56
CD-ROM
    databases, 6-7
    drives, 18
    versus Online, 45-46, 58
Chat e-mail, 87
Command searching, 65
Compatibility, 11
CompuServe, 82
Computerese, 21
Conferences, 60
    selection criteria, 42-44
Content
    accuracy (of electronic
        resources), 40
    need for, 70-71
    value (of electronic
        sources), 40
Costs, 78, 81, 82

Criteria (for selection), 25-36

Databases
    bibliographic, 4-5
    CD-ROM, 6-7
    definition of, 2-3
    directory, 5
    electronic, 2-3
    format of, 33-34
    full text, 4
    hard-disk-resident, 5-6, 68
    indexing of, 26-32
    number and kinds (as selection
        criteria), 80
    online, 6, 75
    organization of, 26-32
    purchased, 76
    types of, 5(chart)
Dates of inclusion, 63
Decision making, 37
Directory databases, 5
Display and printing, 53-54, 62-63
Documentation, 32-33
    and training, 81

E-mail, 86-88
Electrical outlets, 19
Electronic databases, 2-3
Electronic encyclopedia evaluation,
    46-47, 47(chart)
Electronic information resources,
    7(chart)
Electronic information sources, 1
Electronic magazine indexes, 60-63
Electronic resources (selection of),
    7-8
Electronic resources area, 23(chart)